Cooking with Poggi Bonsi

Traveling Through Food

Keli Sim DeRitis

Buon appetito!

Keli Sim DeRitis

First published in 2021

Poggi Bonsi, LLC

ISBN | 978-1-7363022-0-0
ebook ISBN | 978-1-7363022-1-7

Cover design by Keli Sim DeRitis

All photographs by Keli Sim DeRitis with the exception of:
page 8 by Janet Crawley
pages 57 and 104 by Kathy Fox
page 60 by Gerri Tyler
page 74 by Nicholas DeRitis
page 86 Eiffel Tower by Nuno Lopes on Pixabay
page 100 by Harry J. Burgess, Ron Porter, Terry Sayers, and Conger Design on Pixabay

Edited by Kathie Vezzani

For inquiries about this book or to contact the author write to keli@PoggiBonsiGifts.com

First Edition

Printed in South Korea

For Grandma Betty

who shared her love of cooking and taught me
how to knead bread, make jam, and,
"Never trust a skinny cook."
Betty Adamson
1920–1984

Acknowledgements

Many people have helped me in bringing this book to life. It was a longtime dream that would have never been realized without the encouragement and loving support of my family and friends.

Thank you to Mary Pat Iaci for her *sous* chef skills, photo styling assistance, and unwavering enthusiasm. *Merci* to Kathie Vezzani for her editing skills which helped make this book the best it could be. Special thanks to Ellen Gosseen whose wit and grammar expertise brought personality to each recipe.

Most of all, *grazie mille* to my husband, Mark, for always supporting my dreams, and to my sons, Nick and Vince, who are the best cheerleaders, taste-testers, and travel buddies a mom could hope for.

I hope you enjoy all 10 travel-themed menus inspired by my favorite European locales. Gather your family and friends, cook together, and experience new cultures through food with these delicious recipes. We can't always travel, but we can always dream—and eat!

Table of CONTENTS

Ciao!

Thanks for joining me on this culinary adventure. First, let me tell you about myself. I'm an enthusiastic cook, traveler, entrepreneur, and artist. I adore everything about food—cooking it, eating it, depicting it in my art, and sharing it with family and friends. My passion is traveling and experiencing each region's culture through its cuisine—which is why I lead small-group food and wine tours through Italy and France. I love introducing my guests to places that are off the tourist track and dishes that reflect unique culinary traditions.

Some of my earliest memories center around food. Treasure hunts in the Idaho hills picking berries and foraging for mushrooms. Summer afternoons in my Grandma Betty's kitchen, stirring bubbling pots of jam, kneading bread, shaking a Mason jar full of sweet cream to make homemade butter. Then, that first heavenly bite of melting butter and jam slathered on a crusty loaf hot out of the oven. Ahhhhh. It was simple food prepared with love—and these cherished memories shaped my life.

Inspired by this lifelong love of cooking and my enthusiasm for travel, I founded an Italian-themed kitchen shop in 2001 and named it Poggi Bonsi, after the Tuscan town of *Poggibonsi*. Seeking unique products to sell in my shop, I regularly toured the European countryside to attend trade shows and partner with local artisans. During my travels, I also cooked—learning how to make regional specialties from both home cooks and professional chefs in Italy and France. Eventually I began teaching what I learned with cooking classes at Poggi Bonsi. I loved introducing my customers to European culture through food.

Soon friends and customers started asking if they could tag along on my buying trips. This eventually led to an exciting new venture for me: leading tours to Italy and France in 2014. In fact, I eventually closed my beloved kitchen shop in 2017 to concentrate more on my European tour business and cooking classes.

This cookbook was written during the COVID-19 pandemic. Discouraged after having to cancel all of my tours and cooking classes, I needed a project to inspire and focus me while still connecting me to Europe. *Viola! Cooking with Poggi Bonsi* was born. On the following pages, you'll notice that I've included gourmet goodies in my recipes—many imported by my dear friends at Ritrovo Selections. I truly believe in these artisan products. I sold them in my shop and continue to use them in my cooking every day. Because many may not be readily available where you are, I've included resources and substitution suggestions in a product section (pages 170–176) at the back of this book.

I invite you to gather your favorite people and start cooking with Poggi Bonsi. You'll find it's much more fun—and lots easier—to try new recipes together. Let's celebrate the Mediterranean lifestyle one delicious dish at a time.

Buon Appetito!

Keli

Roma

A cultural ritual in restaurants all over Italy, *aperitivo* is derived from the Latin word *aperire* and is meant "to open" the stomach before dining. When you order cocktails in the late afternoon, you're also presented with a selection of little snacks. Offerings can be as simple as peanuts and potato chips, or as elaborate as an extensive appetizer buffet. Imagine being in the eternal city at a quaint *trattoria* with friends, enjoying this tradition—and menu.

Aperitivo
IN ROMA

Spritz Time!

The Aperol Spritz is Italy's iconic drink. Goblets filled with the bubbly orange cocktail—always garnished with fresh orange slices—are served in virtually every bar on the Italian Peninsula. Aperol is a semi-sweet, slightly bitter *aperitif* created in 1919 in northern Italy. In recent years the spritz cocktail has enjoyed worldwide popularity and several alternatives to Aperol have become available. I've recommended a few below—gather your friends and try them all. It's a great excuse for a party!

CLASSIC SPRITZ COCKTAIL

2 ounces Aperol or other bitter orange liqueur
3 ounces Prosecco
1 ounce sparkling water
Orange slice for garnish

1. Fill a goblet with ice, pour in Aperol or other bitter orange liqueur, add Prosecco, and top with sparkling water.
2. Garnish with an orange slice.

Add an ounce of gin to make a "Poggi Spritz."

APEROL

Made in northern Italy, alcohol: 11%, $23–$28

Aperol is a classic Italian bitter *apéritif* made from sweet and bitter oranges, *gentian* (a bitter, astringent, and gastric stimulating herb that reduces inflammation and lowers fevers), rhubarb, *cinchona*, and other ingredients. Its name comes from the French slang word for *aperitif*, which is *apero*. *For more information, visit aperol.com.*

APERIX

Made in Tuscany, Italy, alcohol: 13.5%, $18–$22

Aperix is similar to Aperol with a more friendly price tag and slightly more alcohol. It is made from a proprietary mix of herbs, spices, and fruit essence including *gentian*, rhubarb, *cinchona*, and Mediterranean citrus. *For more information, visit KnightGabriello.it.*

AZZURRO

Made in Burgundy, France, alcohol: 25%, $20–$22

Formulated with less sugar than other liqueurs, it features concentrated herbs including *gentian*, rhubarb, and *cinchona*. Milder than Aperol, the citrus flavors are dominant. With more than twice the alcohol of Aperol, Azzurro packs quite a punch. *For more information, visit PreissImports.com.*

LEOPOLD BROTHERS APERITIVO

Made in Colorado, United States, alcohol: 24%, $35

Following traditional Italian style, this *aperitivo* centers around major flavor components: bitterness from *gentian* root, sweetness from cane sugar, and bright citrus from orange and grapefruit peels. Herbal notes shine through thanks to the addition of fragrant flowering botanicals including hyssop and *Artemsia pontica*. Natural *cochineal* coloring gives Leopold Brothers Aperitivo its vibrant red color. *For more information, visit LeopoldBros.com.*

MARTINI AND ROSSI FIERO

Made in Turin, Italy, alcohol: 15%, $23–$25

Fiero is actually a vermouth, an aromatized wine, not a distilled product as other *aperitivo* liqueurs. It is a blend of white wines and botanicals including *Murcia* orange peel, *Artemisia absinthium*, and *Artemisia pontica*. Complex flavors, sliding from bitter orange peel to notes of cloves and a heavily *gentian*-like character, end with a sweet, brightly fruity finish. *For more information, visit martini.com.*

Angelo Azzurro

The azure hues of the Mediterranean Sea are reflected in this uniquely refreshing "Blue Angel" cocktail.

Makes 1 cocktail

3 ounces gin
1½ ounces triple sec
½ ounce blue curaçao
½ ounce lemon juice, freshly squeezed
Sparkling sugar and lemon slice for garnish

1. Place all ingredients in a cocktail shaker filled with ice and shake vigorously for about 30 seconds.
2. Place sparkling sugar in a shallow saucer. Run a wedge of lemon around the edge of a cocktail glass and dip rim in sugar.
3. Pour into cocktail and garnish with a lemon slice.

Negroni

A cocktail-aficionado friend recently said, "The Negroni is the new martini." This one is stirred, not shaken—and fantastic.

Makes 1 cocktail

1 ounce Campari
1 ounce gin
1 ounce sweet red vermouth such as Giuseppe B. Carpano
Squeeze of fresh orange juice
Orange peel for garnish

1. Fill an old-fashioned glass with ice, pour in Campari, gin, sweet vermouth, and stir.
2. Add a squeeze of fresh orange juice. Garnish with orange slice.

Red-Eye to Roma

Bourbon and wine together in the same cocktail? "*Si, si!*" This drink will take you anywhere, quickly.

Makes 1 cocktail

2 ounces bourbon
1 ounce lemon juice, freshly squeezed
1 ounce simple syrup
1–2 dashes barrel-aged bitters
½ ounce fruity red wine, such as *primitivo*, zinfandel or syrah
Slice of orange, and an Amarena cherry for garnish

1. Pour bourbon, lemon juice, simple syrup, and bitters into a cocktail shaker filled with ice. Shake until outside of shaker is frosty (about 30 seconds). Strain into an old-fashioned glass filled with ice.
2. Gently pour the red wine over the back of a spoon held just above the drink's surface so the wine floats on top.
3. Garnish with a slice of orange and an Amarena cherry.

Simple Syrup

Many cocktails call for sweetening with simple syrup, and it's so easy to make. I like to include fresh herbs as the sugar and water boil to create uniquely flavored syrups—which add layers of taste to alcoholic drinks and "mock-tails" alike.

Makes about 1½ cups

1 cup sugar
1 cup water

1. Place sugar and water in a small saucepan set over medium heat. Bring to a boil and simmer until the sugar is dissolved (about 3 minutes). Remove from the heat and let cool completely.
2. Pour into a sterilized glass container and store in the refrigerator for up to 1 month. It can also be frozen for up to 6 months.
3. Simple syrup is also fantastic when flavored with herbs.
   Variations: add 4–5 sprigs of rosemary or thyme, or a handful of basil to the sugar and water as it boils. Strain before bottling.

Formaggio e Salumi
Cheese and Meat

Italy boasts the largest selection of cheeses in the world—with more than 2,500 traditional varieties—and up to 600 kinds of *salumi*. It would be impossible to list them all, but an ideal range would include two or three types each of cheese and cured meats. I like to start with some arugula on a board or platter, layer on the cheese and meats, then add olives, fruit, or nuts for a colorful presentation.

SOFT CHEESES

Burrata is a decadent cow's milk cheese—the outer shell is solid *mozzarella*, while the inside contains *stracciatella* (bits of *mozzarella*) and cream. It is typical of Puglia, the region situated in the "heel" of the Italian Peninsula. Serve in a ramekin, topped with sliced cherry tomatoes and drizzled with balsamic vinegar.

Buffalo Mozzarella is a quintessential Italian cheese made from the milk of Mediterranean buffalo, and originates in Campania in southern Italy. Cow's milk *mozzarella* is widely available, but the cheese made from buffalo milk has more flavor and is a special treat.

Taleggio is named after Val Taleggio in the Lombardy region of northern Italy. This cheese has a thin crust and strong aroma, but its flavor is mild with a fruity tang that pairs well with fruit.

SEMI-HARD CHEESES

Fontina d'Aosta is a classic Italian cheese with an earthy, nutty flavor, made from cow's milk in the Aosta Valley of northern Italy.

Caciocavallo means "cheese on horseback" and gets its name from the manner in which the cheese is tied together on a rope and hung over a wooden board (resembling a saddle), then left to drain and age. It is similar to *Provolone*, made from cow's milk, and produced throughout southern Italy and in Sicily.

Pecorino di Pienza is sweet, earthy, and pungent. This sheep's cheese from Tuscany is available in three different stages of aging: *fresco*, aged up to 120 days, *stagionati*, aged up to five months, and *riserva*, which is aged up to one year.

HARD CHEESES

Parmigiano-Reggiano or *Parmesan* is a hard, granular cheese made from cow's milk and aged 12–36 months. It is named after the province of Parma-Reggio Emilia where it is made.

Pecorino Romano is not to be confused with P*ecorino di Pienza* or *Pecorino Toscano*. It is a sheep's milk cheese that originates in the Lazio region of central Italy and is aged for at least five months.

BLUE CHEESES

Gorgonzola Dolce is a blue cheese from Lombardy in northern Italy made from cow's milk. Sweet and almost spreadable, its salty pungency pairs beautifully with figs and grapes.

SALUMI

Bresaola is an air-dried, salted beef that has been soaked in wine and spices, then aged two or three months until it becomes hard and turns a dark red color.

Capocollo, *coppa*, or *capicola* is a traditional Italian cold cut made from the dry-cured muscle of the pork shoulder or neck.

Mortadella is a large Italian sausage or luncheon meat made of finely ground heat-cured pork, and incorporates small cubes of pork fat.

Prosciutto is "ham" in Italian. It may be either *crudo* "dry-cured" or *cotto* "cooked."

Soppressata is a Italian dry salami with many variations. A cured dry variety is typical in southern Italy, and an uncured salami is traditional in central Italy.

Ricotta Pinwheels

These showy appetizers are simple to create thanks to purchased puff pastry. Rich *ricotta* with garlic, herbs, and *prosciutto* offer cheesy, salty goodness. Omit the *prosciutto* for a vegetarian option.

Makes about 24 pinwheels

½ cup whole milk *ricotta* cheese
¼ cup, plus 1 tablespoon *Parmigiano-Reggiano* cheese, grated
2 garlic cloves, minced
1 tablespoon fresh rosemary, minced
Sea salt & freshly ground black pepper
1 sheet frozen puff pastry, thawed (see notes)
Unbleached all-purpose flour
4 ounces *prosciutto*

1. Place the *ricotta* cheese, ¼ cup *Parmigiano-Reggiano*, garlic, and rosemary in a small bowl and mix. Add sea salt and freshly ground pepper to taste.
2. Place the puff pastry sheet horizontally on a floured work surface. Roll out into a 10 x 15-inch rectangle, ⅛-inch thick, turning as needed to keep the rectangle even.
3. Lay the *prosciutto* slices on the pastry, leaving about ¾ inch at the bottom edge free.
4. Carefully spread the *ricotta* cheese mixture over the *prosciutto* slices, again leaving the bottom edge free of filling.
5. Starting at the top, slowly roll the pastry downward into a log. Brush the bottom edge with water and press to seal. Wrap in plastic and place in the freezer for at least 1 hour. Pastry can be frozen at this point for up to 3 months.
6. Preheat oven to 400°F and line a baking sheet with parchment paper or a silicone baking mat.
7. Allow pastry to thaw slightly then place seam-side down and slice into ½ to ¾-inch thick rounds and set on the lined baking sheet (about 1 inch apart). Sprinkle with additional *Parmigiano-Reggiano* cheese.
8. Bake for 25–30 minutes, until puffed and golden brown.
9. These are best served on the same day as baked, either warm or at room temperature. They can be stored in the refrigerator in an airtight container for up to 1 week and reheated before serving.

Notes

Puff pastry, also known as *pâté feuilletée*, is a flaky light pastry made from a laminated dough composed of dough and butter or other solid fat.

All puff pastries are not created equally so read the ingredients carefully. Many commercially available pastries are made using palm oil and high fructose corn syrup. I really like Dufour (DufourPastryKitchens.com) a brand made in the European style with sweet cream butter.

Chickpea and Almond Crackers

Looking for gluten-free crackers that don't taste like animal fodder? The ancient Romans had the answer. Their staples—chickpea flour and ground almonds—create deliciously crunchy, naturally gluten-free crackers that are so much more flavorful than commercially produced versions. Once you try them, and see how easy they are to make, you'll never buy gluten-free crackers again. Enjoy these on their own, with salami and cheese, or any other favorite toppings.

Makes about 24 crackers

½ cup chickpea flour (see notes)
½ cup almond flour (almond meal)
1 teaspoon Casina Rossa Herbs&Salt 💜
2 tablespoons extra virgin olive oil 💜
4–6 tablespoons water
Additional extra virgin olive oil and sea salt for top

💜*See favorite products on pages 170–176.*

1. Preheat oven to 400°F and line a baking tray with parchment paper or a silicone baking mat.
2. Place the flours and salt in a large bowl, add 1 tablespoon of extra virgin olive oil and crumble with fingers or mix with a whisk. Slowly add water until the mix comes together and forms a dough. Knead in the bowl for a few minutes until dough is smooth.
3. Form the dough into a flat disk and place between two sheets of parchment paper or a silicone baking mat. Roll dough from center outward, rotate 45° and roll again from the center out (continue all the way around). Flip the parchment and dough over and continue to roll in the same manner until it is about ⅛-inch thick.
4. Remove the top piece of parchment and cut the crackers into desired shapes with a cookie cutter or a pastry wheel. Gather any scraps and re-roll until all dough is used.
5. Carefully transfer crackers to the prepared baking sheet, perforate each cracker with a fork, brush with extra virgin olive oil, and sprinkle with sea salt (other flavored salts are good for this too).
6. Bake for 10–15 minutes, until they are slightly golden. Allow to cool for a few minutes before serving. Store crackers in an airtight container in the refrigerator for up to 1 week, or in the freezer for up to 3 months.

Notes

Flour made from chickpeas or *garbanzo* beans has been used in Middle Eastern, Indian, French, and Italian cuisines for centuries.

Chickpeas are one of the earliest cultivated legumes. Remains of this ancient bean have been found in the Middle East dating back 7,500 years!

Lamb Meatballs

Ground lamb gives these cocktail-sized meatballs a rich, earthy flavor; my addition of pine nuts and golden raisins enhances the texture and adds just a touch of sweetness. I like to serve them both as an appetizer or tossed with freshly-cooked pasta.

Makes about 36 meatballs

For the sauce:
2 tablespoons extra virgin olive oil
1 small white onion, chopped
3 garlic cloves, sliced
One 28-ounce can *San Marzano* tomatoes ♥
2 teaspoons fresh oregano leaves, or 1 teaspoon dried oregano

For the meatballs:
1 pound ground lamb
¼ cup pine nuts, whole
¼ cup golden raisins, finely chopped
¼ cup freshly grated *Parmigiano-Reggiano* cheese, grated
¼ cup unseasoned bread crumbs
3 large eggs
2 medium garlic cloves, minced
1 teaspoon Casina Rossa Herbs&Salt ♥
1 teaspoon Fior di Maiella Spicy Bruschetta Salt ♥
Extra virgin olive oil as needed for sautéing

♥*See favorite products section on pages 170–176.*

For the sauce:
1. In a medium saucepan set over medium-high heat, add the olive oil, onion, and garlic. Sauté until soft, about 5 minutes.
2. Add the tomatoes and oregano and simmer, for about 10 minutes until the flavors blend. Set aside.

For the meatballs:
3. Place the lamb, pine nuts, raisins, *Parmigiano-Reggiano* cheese, bread crumbs, eggs, garlic, Herbs&Salt, and Spicy *Bruschetta* Salt in a large bowl; mix well.
4. Form meatballs using about 1 tablespoon of the meat mixture for each one. A small cookie scoop is ideal for this. Smaller or larger meatballs can be made if desired.
5. Pour about ¼ inch of olive oil in a large skillet set over medium heat. Once the oil begins to smoke, add the meatballs and sauté, turning frequently, until they are browned on all sides and the interior temperature is 135°F (about 10 minutes). Meatballs can also be baked in a mini muffin pan in the oven at 350°F for 15–20 minutes.
6. Transfer the meatballs to the pan with the sauce and simmer for about 1 hour. Serve with toothpicks as an appetizer or toss with pasta. Meatballs can be stored in the refrigerator for 3–5 days or in the freezer for up to 3 months.

Pairing suggestion: Nero d'Avola, Chianti Classico, or Rosso dell'Umbria

Saltimbocca Chicken Bites

Chunks of tender chicken breast wrapped in sage and *prosciutto*, then topped with *Parmigiano-Reggiano* cheese.... Now you can savor all the deliciousness of *Saltimbocca* in one tasty bite!

Makes 12–16 appetizers

1 large chicken breast
1 bunch fresh sage
4 ounces *prosciutto*
Extra virgin olive oil for frying
Sea salt
***Parmigiano-Reggiano* cheese, grated**
Toothpicks for securing

Prepare the chicken bites:
1. Cut the chicken breast into 1-inch chunks.
2. Remove sage leaves from stalk; wash and set aside to dry.
3. Cut *prosciutto* slices in half vertically.
4. Fold 1 sage leaf around a chunk of chicken, then carefully wrap a *prosciutto* slice over the leaf around the chicken, and secure through the middle with a toothpick. Repeat for all of the chicken pieces and set aside.

Fry the sage leaves:
5. Place 3–4 tablespoons of extra virgin olive oil in a heavy skillet set over medium heat.
6. Drop remaining sage leaves into the oil; do not overcrowd. Sauté for a minute or two on each side, just until sage leaves turn dark (be careful not to burn them). Set aside to drain on paper towels and sprinkle with sea salt. Reserve the oil which is now infused with sage.

Fry the Saltimbocca bites:
7. Add the chicken bites to the pan and sauté 4–5 minutes on each side, until brown and crispy.
8. Remove to a serving dish and top with *Parmigiano-Reggiano* cheese and fried sage leaves.

Pairing suggestion: Prosecco, Pinot Grigio, Chianti

Notes

Frying sage leaves mellows and sweetens their flavor. Delicious as a stand-alone appetizer, they also add a special touch to pasta dishes and grilled meats.

Smoked Pepper Pecorino Shortbread

These lovely shortbread crackers are smoky, sharp, and salty—with lots of crunch from the cheese and poppy seeds, plus a beautiful color thanks to the addition of the smoked sweet pepper. A treat on their own, they're also especially nice served with soft cheeses such as *Brie* or *Camembert*.

Makes 24 crackers

1 cup unbleached all-purpose flour
½ cup unsalted butter, cubed
4 ounces *Pecorino Romano* cheese, grated
½ teaspoon sea salt
1 tablespoon Fior di Maiella Smoked Sweet Pepper Powder 💜
2–3 tablespoons poppy seeds
1 tablespoon water, if needed

💜*See favorite products section on pages 170–176.*

1. Place all the ingredients in the bowl of a food processor and pulse until the mixture resembles bread crumbs. Add 1 tablespoon of cold water if needed to bring the ingredients together.
2. Tip the dough out onto a board and knead until a smooth ball forms. Form the dough into a log about 1½-inch diameter, then roll in poppy seeds.
3. Wrap in plastic wrap and chill for at least an hour. (Dough can be frozen for up to 3 months and thawed slightly before slicing and baking.)
4. Preheat the oven to 350°F and line a baking sheet with parchment paper or a silicone baking mat.
5. Slice the dough into ¼-inch thick rounds and transfer to the baking sheet. Bake for 12–14 minutes, until the edges are slightly brown.
6. Let cool on a wire rack before serving. Store in an airtight container for up to 2 weeks, or freeze for up to 3 months.

Pairing suggestion: Prosecco, Zinfandel (Primitivo)

Notes

You can also use *Parmigiano-Reggiano* cheese in this recipe, which will result in a tasty cracker that is a bit milder in flavor.

Suppli di Riso con Funghi e Fontina

Roman Rice Croquettes

Suppli are simply the baby brothers of *arancini*, the giant rice croquettes from Sicily. My version is made with mushroom *risotto* and *Fontina* cheese—but use any flavor of leftover *risotto* you have. Some of my favorite combinations are tomato basil *risotto* with *mozzarella*, and butternut squash *risotto* with *Gorgonzola*.

Makes about 36 suppli

For the mushroom risotto:
4–6 cups low-sodium vegetable or chicken broth (or as much as needed)
2 tablespoons extra virgin olive oil
1 sweet onion, diced
1 pound package *Carnaroli* or *Arborio* rice
1 cup dry white wine
3 cups *crimini* mushrooms, finely chopped
½ cup heavy cream
1 tablespoon Casina Rossa Truffle&Salt ♥
½ cup grated *Parmigiano-Reggiano* cheese
Salt and freshly ground black pepper

For the suppli:
6 ounces *Fontina* cheese, cut into ½-inch chunks
1 cup unbleached all-purpose flour
2 eggs beaten with ⅓ cup whole milk
2 cups bread crumbs
Oil for frying (safflower, coconut, or peanut)

♥ *See favorite products section on pages 170–176.*

For the mushroom risotto:

1. Pour the broth into a medium saucepan set over low heat.
2. Pour the extra virgin olive oil into a large *risotto* or stew pot set over medium heat. Add the onion and sauté until translucent (about 5 minutes). Add the rice and, stirring constantly, toasting for about 1 minute.
3. Add wine and stir until fully absorbed. Add the mushrooms and cook at a slow simmer, adding heated broth ½ cupful at a time. Stir continually, making sure the *risotto* absorbs the liquid before adding more and does not stick to the bottom. As the rice continues to absorb the liquid, it will become tender and creamy.
4. Use 4–6 cups broth, more or less as needed. It usually takes about 20 minutes for the *risotto* to become completely cooked. It should be wonderfully creamy and thick—it's best *al dente*, which means the rice should retain some firmness when you chew it. Add the heavy cream and Truffle&Salt, stirring well to combine.
5. Remove from heat; stir in the *Parmigiano-Reggiano* cheese. Season with additional sea salt and freshly ground pepper to taste.
6. Serve right away with additional *Parmigiano-Reggiano* cheese, or refrigerate for at least 8 hours and make the *suppli*.

For the suppli:

7. Wet hands slightly and take a walnut-sized portion of the *risotto* and create an indentation in the center. Insert a piece of cheese and wrap the *risotto* around it, patting with fingers to form an oval shape. Repeat with remaining *risotto* and set aside.
8. Place the flour in a shallow bowl, whisk the eggs and milk in another, and place the bread crumbs in a third bowl.
9. Roll each rice ball in the flour, then in the egg mixture, and finally roll in bread crumbs until evenly coated. Continue with remaining *suppli*.
10. Pour about 2 inches of oil into a heavy saucepan set over medium heat until it reaches 350°F.
11. Using a slotted spoon, gently transfer 4–5 *suppli* at a time into the oil and fry until golden brown (5–7 minutes), turning halfway through.
12. Remove from oil and drain on paper towels. Serve warm or refrigerate for up to 5 days and reheat in the oven. *Suppli* can also be frozen for up to 6 months and reheated.

Biscotti di Cioccolato e Nocciole

Chocolate Hazelnut Biscotti

Biscotti means "twice-cooked" in Italian, and these crispy cookies make the perfect finale to our *aperitivo* buffet—and everything else! Full of rich coffee flavor, chocolate chunks, and hazelnuts, they are wonderful when dunked into piping hot *espresso*. I like to serve them with a scoop or two of *gelato*.

Makes about 36 biscotti

1 cup hazelnuts (or walnuts)
2¾ cups unbleached all-purpose flour
½ cup unsweetened cocoa powder
2 tablespoons *espresso* powder
   (see notes)
1½ teaspoon baking powder
¼ teaspoon sea salt
½ cup unsalted butter, softened
1 cup sugar
3 eggs, at room temperature
1 teaspoon vanilla extract
1 teaspoon almond extract
1 cup dark chocolate, cut into chunks,
   or chocolate chips

Notes

Instant coffee granules can also be used. Grind them into a fine powder with a grinder, mini food processor, or mortar and pestle.

1. Preheat oven to 325°F. Position rack in the center of oven.
2. Line baking sheet with parchment paper or a silicone baking mat.
3. Spread hazelnuts on the baking sheet and toast in oven for about 12–15 minutes, or until skins begin to crack. Wrap nuts in a kitchen towel and allow to rest for a few minutes. Rub hazelnuts together in the towel to remove skins (which can be composted). Let cool for a bit, then chop coarsely and set aside.
4. Increase the oven temperature to 350°F.
5. In a medium bowl, whisk together the flour, cocoa powder, *espresso* powder, baking powder, and salt. Set aside.
6. In the bowl of an electric stand mixer fitted with paddle attachment, beat the butter and sugar until fluffy.
7. Beat in the eggs, 1 at a time.
8. Add vanilla and almond extracts.
9. With the mixer on low speed, add the flour mixture a little at a time, until incorporated (do not overmix). Stir in the toasted hazelnuts and chocolate.
10. Divide dough into thirds and form each piece into a 2 x 10-inch log (it's easier to form with wet fingers).
11. Bake for approximately 25–30 minutes or until firm to the touch. Transfer the baking sheet to a rack and let cool slightly.
12. Transfer each cookie log to a cutting board and, using a serrated knife, slice cookies ½ to ¾-inch thick. It helps to press down gently at first and then slice with the knife. For larger cookies, cut at an angle.
13. Place the sliced cookies back on the baking sheet, and bake for an additional 20–30 minutes, turning them over halfway through. The longer the cookies cook, the crispier they will be.
14. *Biscotti* can be stored in an airtight container for up to 1 week.

Pairing suggestion: Espresso, Lambrusco di Sorbara, late harvest Zinfandel, or Recioto

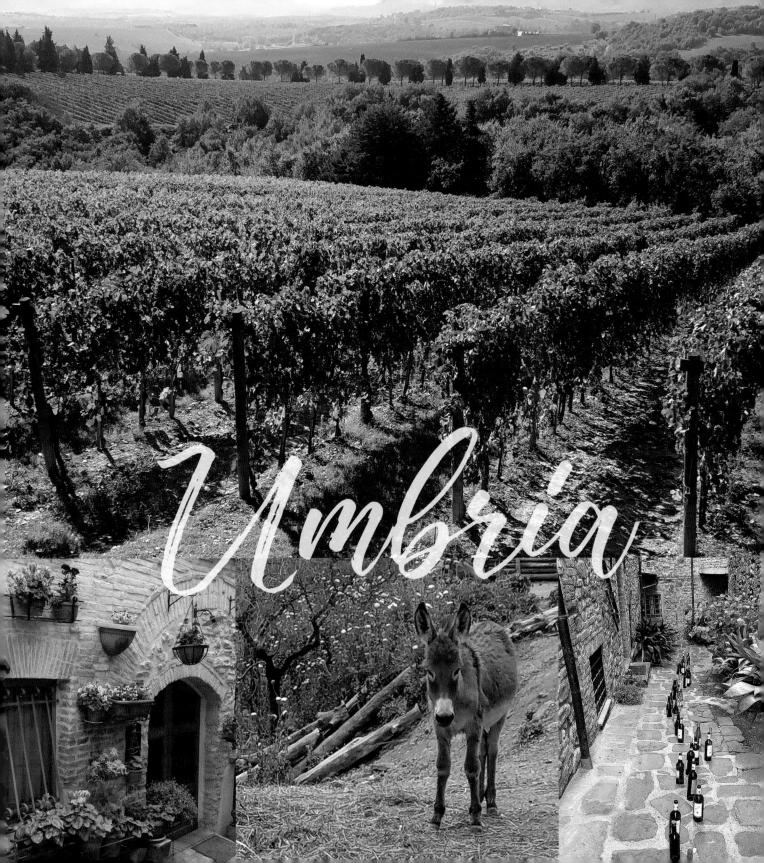

Umbria

Considered the "Green Heart of Italy," Umbria holds a special place in my heart. Being the only land-locked region on the Italian Peninsula, the landscape is full of rolling hills studded with vineyards, nut trees, and oak forests. This menu celebrates both Umbria and the flavors of my favorite time of year—when the air turns crisp and I relish a day spent in my kitchen cooking for family and friends.

Autumn
IN UMBRIA

Fig Thyme Fizz

The marriage of figs and thyme adds fruity, herbaceous flavor and lovely color to this refreshing cocktail.

Makes 1 cocktail

For the shrub (see notes):
1 pound fresh figs, roughly chopped
1 cup sugar
4–5 sprigs of fresh thyme
½ cup Ritrovo Selections White Balsamic Vinegar ♥

For the cocktail:
½–1 ounce Fig Shrub (see notes)
2 ounces vodka
1 ounce *limoncello*
Splash of sparkling water
Fresh fig and thyme for garnish

♥*See favorite products section on pages 170–176.*

For the shrub:
1. Place figs, sugar, and thyme in a glass bowl and stir. Cover with plastic wrap and leave at room temperature for 24 hours (overnight), stirring occasionally to make sure all the sugar has dissolved.
2. Strain the fig mixture through a fine mesh sieve, reserve the liquid and compost the figs. Add the vinegar to the liquid and store in a sterilized glass container in the refrigerator for up to 1 month. Shrubs can also be frozen up to 3 months in jars or ice cube trays.

For the cocktail:
3. Fill a cocktail glass with ice, pour in the fig shrub, vodka, and *limoncello* and stir. Top with a splash of sparkling water.
4. Garnish with a fresh fig and sprig of thyme.

Notes

A "shrub" is a mixture of fresh fruit, sugar, and vinegar—and has been used for centuries as a way to preserve fruit juice.

Shrubs can be made with any type of fruit and vinegar. It's not necessary to add herbs, but adding them enhances the flavor.

Other combinations to try are strawberry/basil, pear/rosemary, blueberry/lavender, raspberry/lemon verbena, and melon/mint. Put on your witch's hat and have some fun concocting.

Baked Pecorino with Figs

This recipe uses *Pecorino di Pienza fresco* cheese, but you can also use *Asiago* or *Cambozola* with delicious results. Serve with crackers or *baguette* slices—yum!

Serves 4

6 ounces *Pecorino di Pienza fresco* cheese (see notes)
2–3 figs, quartered
1 teaspoon fresh thyme leaves
¼ cup hazelnuts, toasted
1 tablespoon ADI Apicoltura Organic Orange Flower Honey ♥

♥*See favorite products section on pages 170–176.*

1. Preheat oven to 400°F.
2. Cut the *Pecorino* into pieces and arrange in a small oven-proof dish. Arrange figs and hazelnuts on top and sprinkle with thyme leaves, then drizzle with the honey.
3. Bake for 12–15 minutes or until bubbly and golden.
4. Serve with Olive Oil Crackers (recipe on page 32) or Classic *Baguette* (recipe on page 141) slices.

Notes

Pecorino di Pienza fresco is a sheep's milk cheese from Tuscany that is aged for only 30 days. It is not widely available in the U.S., but can be found at many Italian specialty stores and online.

Pienza is a Tuscan village famous for its *Pecorino* cheese and perfect design (thanks to Pope Pius II). *Pecorino di Pienza* can be found in three different styles: *fresco*, aged up to 120 days, *stagionato*, aged up to 5 months, and *riserva*, which is aged up to 1 year.

Olive Oil Crackers

Crispy and flavorful, these crackers are wonderful paired with cheeses or dips. This recipe is essentially a pasta dough with a little seasoning. Using a pasta machine helps get the dough to the desired thinness, but you can also achieve great results with a rolling pin and a little elbow grease.

Makes about 48 crackers

1 cup "00" ♥ (see notes) or
    unbleached all-purpose flour
1 cup semolina flour, plus more
    for dusting
1 tablespoon sugar
1 teaspoon Casina Rossa Herbs&Salt ♥
⅔ cup warm water
3 tablespoons extra virgin olive oil,
    plus more for brushing
1 teaspoon flake sea salt

*♥See favorite products section
on pages 170–176.*

Notes

"00" flour is Italian milled flour that is used for pasta and pastry making. You will find that this is also called *Doppio Zero* which means "double zero" in Italian. The grading system is 2, 1, 0 or 00, indicating how finely ground the flour is and how much of the bran and germ have been removed.

1. Place all-purpose flour, semolina flour, sugar, and Herbs&Salt in a large bowl; whisk until well combined. Add warm water and extra virgin olive oil, then mix thoroughly. Once the dough comes together, turn it out onto a board and knead for 6 minutes until it is smooth and elastic.

2. Form the dough into a ball and wrap with plastic wrap and allow to sit at room temperature for 1 hour. (The dough can be made ahead at this point and stored in the refrigerator for up to 2 days.)

3. Preheat the oven to 400°F. Line two baking sheets with parchment paper or silicone baking mats. Divide the dough into 4 equal-sized balls. Dust 1 ball with semolina flour and flatten it into a disk about ½-inch thick. Run the dough through a pasta roller on the widest setting. Fold the ends of the dough toward the center into thirds (as you would a letter), and feed it through the rollers with the open end first. (This will help make the edges of the crackers stay even.)

4. Continue feeding the dough through the machine once for each setting, adjusting the roller to the next-thinner setting each time until the dough is about 1/16-inch thick (#5 setting on most pasta rollers). Alternately, roll each dough ball with a rolling pin until it's a long 1/16-inch-thick sheet. Lay the sheet of dough out on a board and, using a pastry cutter or sharp knife, cut the dough crosswise into 1½-inch sections. Carefully transfer the crackers to the prepared baking sheets.

5. Brush each cracker with extra virgin olive oil and sprinkle with flake sea salt. Bake until they are golden brown and crisp (about 10–12 minutes), rotating the baking sheets once from top to bottom and from back to front while baking. Watch crackers carefully because they can burn quickly. Repeat with the remaining dough to make 4 more cracker sheets. Crackers can be stored in a sealed container for up to 1 week.

Marmellata di Pomodorini

Cherry Tomato Jam

A sweet and savory condiment for meats or cheeses, this unique jam is also especially tasty on sandwiches.

Makes 1½ pints

1 tablespoon extra virgin olive oil
1 large shallot, chopped (about ⅓ cup)
3 garlic cloves, minced
1 teaspoon Fior di Maiella Smoked
    Sweet Pepper Powder ♥
⅛ teaspoon Michele Ferrante
    Controne Hot Pepper ♥
4 cups cherry tomatoes
2 tablespoons Ritrovo Selections
    Tomato Balsamic Vinegar ♥
2 tablespoons ADI Apicoltura Organic
    Orange Flower Honey ♥
1 teaspoon thyme leaves
1 teaspoon sea salt

♥ *See favorite products section on pages 170–176.*

1. Heat the olive oil in a large non-reactive pot over medium heat. Add the shallot and garlic; saute for 3–5 minutes until softened.
2. Add the smoked pepper powder and *Controne* pepper flakes, then sauté 30 seconds more.
3. Add the tomatoes, tomato balsamic, honey, thyme leaves, and sea salt and bring to a boil. Reduce heat to medium low and simmer, stirring often (about 10–15 minutes), until the tomatoes burst and thicken. Mash the tomatoes with a wooden spoon.
4. Remove from heat and season with additional sea salt and red pepper flakes, if desired. Transfer to sterilized jars and seal the tops. Let rest at room temperature overnight. Jam can be stored in the refrigerator for 10–14 days or frozen for up to 6 months.

Marmellata di Prugne

Italian Plum Jam

Makes about 1 pint

3 pounds ripe Italian plums, rinsed,
    pitted, and halved
1 cup sugar
Juice of 1 lemon

1. Place plum halves in a large mixing bowl and sprinkle with sugar. Stir until plums are evenly coated with sugar. Let them sit for 1 hour then transfer to a heavy non-reactive pot.
2. Set pot over medium heat, bring mixture to a boil uncovered, stirring occasionally. Boil until the mixture is bubbling uniformly. Remove from heat and allow to cool.
3. Transfer jam to the bowl of a food processor and pulse until puréed. Return to the pot set over medium heat and cook until jam is reduced. To test if it's ready, spoon a little of the hot jam onto a cold saucer and place in the freezer for 2 minutes or until chilled. Touch the jam; if it wrinkles and feels gel-like, it's ready to be transferred into sterilized jars. Jam will keep in the refrigerator for up to 1 month, or in the freezer for up to 6 months.

Torta al Testo

Umbrian Panini

Torta al testo, also known as *crescia*, is a traditional skillet bread from Umbria. Its origins date back to the Roman Empire, when these round flat breads were cooked on a large brick disc called a *testum*. Today, the name *testo* refers to the cast iron pan on which the *torta* is cooked—a large cast iron skillet works well too. Steamed chard and cheese is a popular filling, but I prefer meat with cheese. I was first introduced to this wonderful dish by my friend Chef Jennifer McIlvaine of *LifeItalianStyle.com*.

Serves 4–8

For the torta:
2½ cups "00" ♥ or unbleached
    all-purpose flour
2 tablespoons baking powder
¼ teaspoon baking soda
1 teaspoon sea salt
1 cup warm water
3 tablespoons extra virgin olive oil
3 tablespoons *Parmigiano-Reggiano*
    cheese

For the filling:
½ cup Cherry Tomato Jam (recipe
    on page 33)
2 balls fresh *mozzarella* cheese, sliced
12–16 slices *prosciutto*
Arugula

♥*See favorite products section on pages 170–176.*

For the torta:
1. Sift the flour, baking powder, baking soda, and sea salt into a large bowl.
2. Make a well in the center, add water, and mix well.
3. Add the olive oil and *Parmigiano-Reggiano* cheese and mix well. Knead the dough for about 10 minutes, wrap in plastic and let rest at room temperature for 30–60 minutes.
4. Divide the dough into 2 balls, and roll out into a round *"pizza"* shape.
5. Set a heavy cast iron skillet over medium-high heat (do not add oil to the pan). Place 1 dough round in the hot pan and poke a few times with a fork. When it begins to turn dark brown (about 5 minutes), flip and continue cooking until the other side is dark brown, then remove from heat. Repeat with the other ball of dough.

For the filling:
6. Let the bread cool for a few minutes. Using a serrated bread knife, slice in half horizontally and spread one half with ¼ cup of the Cherry Tomato Jam. Arrange half of the *mozzarella* on the other slice, top with half of the *prosciutto* slices, and a mound of arugula. Top with the jam-coated piece, cut into quarters and serve warm. *Panini* can be wrapped in foil and stored in the refrigerator for 3–5 days and reheated to serve.

Pairing suggestion: Umbrian Sangiovese blend such as Roccascossa Umbria IGT by Terre Margaritelli

Notes

Any combination of *salumi*, cheese, and greens can be used as fillings so have some fun and experiment.

Pici Pasta

Grazie to my friend Colleen Simpson, owner of the glorious vacation home *L'Antica Vetreria*—a restored glass factory in Umbria (*AnticaVetreria.net*), for sharing her *pici* pasta recipe. Also called *stringozzi*, *pici* is a thick *spaghetti* traditionally made with a *chitarra*—a guitar-like pasta-making tool. A pasta press with the *spaghetti* roller works too. Enjoy this pasta with any sauce, although I find it especially delicious with Wild Boar *Ragù* (recipe on page 38).

Serves 8–12

4 cups "00" ♥ or unbleached all-purpose flour
3 large eggs
¼ cup sunflower oil (do not use olive oil)
1 tablespoon sea salt, plus additional for cooking
¾ cup water, room temperature (more or less may be needed to create a firm dough)
Semolina flour for dusting

♥ *See favorite products section on pages 170–176.*

Make the pasta:

1. Place flour on a clean work surface, form a well or "volcano" in the center. Add the salt and oil in the well. While whisking with a fork, add 1 egg at a time, working the flour into the mixture. Work with hands to mix together. A bench scraper is a good tool to scrape surface and form dough. Slowly begin to add water, continuing to work with hands to mix. Add more water as necessary to create a firm dough. If you add too much water, it is easy to correct—simply add more flour.

2. Knead the dough until it is smooth and elastic, but firm (about 10 minutes). Add flour as necessary to keep dough from sticking to the work surface. Wrap the dough in plastic wrap and allow to rest for at least 30 minutes.

3. Sprinkle semolina flour onto a baking sheet and set aside.

4. Form the dough into a log about 3 inches thick and cut into 1½-inch segments. Place one segment on work surface and liberally dust with all-purpose flour to prevent it from sticking. Using a rolling pin, roll the segment into a long rectangle about ⅛-inch thick. Trim the rectangle 3 inches shorter than the *chitarra*. Reserve the trimmings and then re-roll them.

5. Place the dough on the *chitarra* and roll firmly with rolling pin until dough drops through the wire. (If using a pasta press, roll to ⅛-inch thick and pass through the *spaghetti* cutter.)

6. Dust the pasta strands with semolina flour, and twist into a little mound and allow to rest on the prepared baking sheet. The pasta can be cooked immediately or frozen on the baking sheet for 1 hour or until firm, then transferred to an airtight container and frozen for up to 3 months.

Cook the pasta:

7. Set a large pot half full of water seasoned with 1–2 tablespoons of sea salt over medium heat. Bring to a rolling boil.

8. Add the pasta and then immediately begin to stir it gently so that the noodles do not stick together. Continue to cook until the pasta is *al dente* (cooked through, but firm: about 3–5 minutes for fresh and 5–7 minutes for frozen).

Ragù di Cinghiale

Wild Boar Ragù

This exotic pasta sauce is rich and satisfying. With a unique flavor that tastes like a combination of beef and pork, wild boar is available at specialty butchers and online. You can also use other wild game such as elk and venison in this recipe. Domestic pork or lamb makes a tasty substitution as well—you just won't need to marinate it prior to making the *ragù*.

Serves 6–8

For the marinade:
**2–3 pounds wild boar leg or shoulder
    meat cubed into bite-sized pieces**
**1 bottle dry Italian red wine such
    as** *Sangiovese*
2 carrots, diced
2 garlic cloves, whole
12 juniper berries, crushed with a knife
½ yellow onion, diced
1 bay leaf

For the wild boar ragù:
2–3 pounds marinated wild boar
2–4 tablespoons extra virgin olive oil
1 medium sweet onion, diced
3–4 garlic cloves, minced
1 cup Italian parsley leaves
**1 cup hearty red wine
    like a** *Sangiovese* **blend**
1 28-ounce can *San Marzano*
    tomatoes ♥
2 sprigs fresh rosemary
10–12 fresh sage leaves
**1–2 teaspoons Casina Rossa
    Herbs&Salt ♥**
Michele Ferrante *Controne*
    Hot Pepper ♥
***Parmigiano-Reggiano* cheese**
Fresh parsley, finely chopped

*♥See favorite products section
on pages 170–176.*

For the marinade:
1. Place wild boar pieces in a large, non-reactive container. Pour over the wine, add carrots, garlic, juniper berries, onions and bay leaf. Gently mix to combine. Allow to marinate in the refrigerator for 24 hours.

For the wild boar ragù:
2. Drain the marinade from the meat and discard.
3. Place the oil, onion, and minced garlic in a large heavy skillet set over medium heat and cook until the onion is golden at the edges (about 10 minutes). Add the meat, stir, and cook until browned (about 5 more minutes). Add the parsley and wine, stir, and bring the wine to a boil. Reduce the heat so the wine is simmering and cook, stirring occasionally, until the meat has absorbed most of the wine (about 25 minutes).
4. Add the tomatoes, stirring to combine, then add the rosemary, sage, Herbs&Salt, and hot pepper flakes if desired. Bring the juices to a boil, reduce the heat, cover and cook until the meat is very tender and has absorbed almost all the liquid (about 2 hours). Check the meat occasionally and stir so that it doesn't stick and break up the tomatoes into smaller pieces.
6. To serve, place a swirl of *pici* (recipe on page 38) or other pasta in a serving bowl and spoon a large portion of the *ragù* over the pasta. Then sprinkle with fresh parsley and freshly grated *Parmigiano-Reggiano* cheese.

Pairing suggestion: Any Sangiovese blend including Chianti Classico, Brunello di Montalcino, or a Super Tuscan

Pork Tenderloin "Porchetta"

Porchetta is a succulent pork roast found in virtually every village market and *macelleria* (butcher shop) in central Italy. The roast is deboned, stuffed with more pork, rolled with wild fennel and herbs, then roasted over a wood fire for at least 8 hours. My version is less labor-intensive and uses a butterflied pork tenderloin, stuffed with ground pork, bread crumbs, and fresh herbs.

Serves 8

1 center-cut pork loin (about 3 pounds)
1–2 tablespoons Casina Rossa Herbs&Salt ♥, divided
4 ounces *prosciutto*
⅓ cup extra virgin olive oil, divided
1 medium onion, finely chopped
3 garlic cloves, minced
½ pound ground pork
1 cup bread crumbs
1 tablespoon fresh rosemary, finely chopped
1 tablespoon fresh thyme, finely chopped
2 teaspoons fresh sage, finely chopped
½ teaspoon pepper
½ cup white wine
Ritrovo Selections Apple Balsamic Vinegar ♥

♥*See favorite products section on pages 170–176.*

1. Preheat oven to 375°F.
2. Butterfly the pork tenderloin. Place loin on a cutting board, hold a knife blade parallel to the board and make a lengthwise cut about ⅓ of the way from the bottom of the pork, stopping about 1 inch from the opposite end. Be careful not to cut through. Open the loin like a book. Make a second cut into the thick side of the pork, parallel to the first cut. Do not cut all the way through; stop about 1 inch from the opposite edge. Fold open to make one long cut of pork tenderloin.
3. Place a piece of plastic wrap under and one piece over the entire tenderloin; pound to an even ⅜-inch thickness.
4. Season both sides with Herbs&Salt (about 1 teaspoon per side).
5. Arrange the *prosciutto* slices horizontally on top of the tenderloin, overlapping slightly. Set aside.
6. Place 2 tablespoons of the olive oil in a large skillet set over medium heat. Add onions and cook until transparent (about 5 minutes). Add garlic and sauté a few minutes more. Add ground pork and cook, stirring occasionally, until browned (about 10–15 minutes).
7. Add the remaining olive oil, bread crumbs, herbs, 1–2 teaspoons of Herbs&Salt, pepper, and white wine. Cook until the wine is absorbed. Set aside to cool slightly.
8. Lay the stuffing over the *prosciutto* slices, leaving about ½ inch free at one side.
9. Gently roll the tenderloin like a jelly roll, starting with the end opposite the ½-inch margin. Using the plastic wrap to fold over the pork makes this a little easier. Arrange the seam side down and tie with baker's twine at ¾-inch intervals.
10. Heat a large oven-proof skillet over medium-high heat and sear the tenderloin on all sides. Cook 2–3 minutes on each side until browned all the way around.
11. Place skillet in the oven and bake for 20–25 minutes until internal temperature reaches 145°F. Remove from oven, cover with foil and allow to rest 5 minutes.
12. Remove the baker's string and cut the pork into ¾-inch slices.
13. Serve on a mound of sautéed Fennel and Apples (recipe on page 42) drizzled with Ritrovo Selections Apple Balsamic. *"Porchetta"* will keep in the refrigerator for up to 5 days.

Pairing suggestion: Italian Barbera

Finocchi e Mele

Sautéed Fennel and Apples

Once you taste this sautéed fennel and apples with apple balsamic, you'll want to pair it with everything pork—especially the Pork Tenderloin *"Porchetta"* on page 41.

Serves 8

2 apples, peeled and cored (see notes)
2 fennel bulbs
¼ cup unsalted butter
1 teaspoon Casina Rossa Herbs&Salt ♥
2 tablespoons Ritrovo Selections Apple Balsamic Vinegar ♥

♥*See favorite products section on pages 170–176.*

Notes

Any kind of apples can be used in this dish, but Golden Delicious and Honeycrisp are especially nice with the fennel.

1. Using a *mandoline* or sharp knife, slice apples and fennel bulb into ⅛-inch slices.
2. Melt butter in a heavy skillet set over medium heat. Add the apple and fennel slices; sauté until tender and slightly browned (about 10 minutes).
3. Season with Herbs&Salt and stir in Apple Balsamic. Continue to cook until the apple and fennel are caramelized.
4. Can be stored in the refrigerator for up to 5 days.

Fagiolini Bagna Càuda
Green Beans with Anchovies and Garlic

Bagna Càuda means "hot bath" in northern Italian dialect. Anchovies, garlic, and olive oil are cooked until the anchovies melt, and then served as a *pinzimonio* "dip" for assorted fresh vegetables. Say, "*Arrivederci!*" to boring beans—this sauce transforms them into a unique and exciting side dish.

Serves 8

1½ pounds *haricots verts* (petit green beans)
¼ cup extra virgin olive oil
6–8 anchovy fillets
4–6 garlic cloves
Zest and juice of 1 lemon
⅛ teaspoon Michele Ferrante *Controne* Hot Pepper ♥ (optional)
Lemon wedges dipped in hot pepper flakes for serving

♥*See favorite products section on pages 170–176.*

1. Blanch the green beans in boiling water for 3–4 minutes, then immerse in ice water to stop cooking.
2. Place the olive oil in a heavy skillet set over medium-high heat. Add the anchovy fillets and cook until melted (3–4 minutes). Add garlic and sauté for a few minutes more, then add the lemon zest and juice.
3. Add the green beans and cook until just heated through.
4. Serve the beans with the sauce drizzled on top. Beans will keep in the refrigerator for 5 days. Leftovers make a nice addition to green salads.

Notes

The *Bagna Càuda sauce is also delicious with broccoli, broccoli rabe, and asparagus.*

Crostata di Marmellata

Jam Tart

This traditional Italian tart recipe is so versatile! Any fruit jam can be used, although plum and apricot are my personal favorites. Enjoy as a delicious dessert with ice cream, or for breakfast with *espresso*.

Serves 8–10

3½ cups "00" ♥ or unbleached
    all-purpose flour
1 cup confectioners' sugar
1 tablespoon orange zest
1 cup butter, cold, cut into chunks
3 eggs
1¼ cup plum jam (recipe on page 33)
1 tablespoon heavy cream
Sugar for topping

♥*See favorite products on pages 170–176.*

1. Place flour, sugar, and orange zest in the bowl of a food processor; pulse until thoroughly mixed.
2. With the processor on, add the butter chunks 1 at a time and pulse until the dough resembles cornmeal.
3. Add the eggs 1 at a time, pulsing in between each egg, until the dough almost forms a ball.
4. Turn the dough out onto a lightly-floured board and gently form the dough into a ball. Wrap in plastic wrap and place in the refrigerator for at least 1 hour.
5. Preheat oven to 350°F. Remove dough from the refrigerator and cut into 2 pieces, one slightly larger than the other. Place the larger dough ball on a heavily-floured board and, using a rolling pin, roll out the dough until it is about ⅛-inch thick.
6. Roll the dough on to the rolling pin, and transfer it to an 11-inch tart pan with a removable bottom, patting it firmly into the pan.
7. Spread jam evenly over the crust.
8. Roll out the smaller ball of dough to ⅛-inch thickness and cut ½ to ¾-inch strips with a pastry roller. Lay strips of dough across the tart in one direction, turn the tart pan slightly and lay the remaining strips of dough over the jam to make a lattice pattern on the *crostata*. Press the edges of the pastry strips into the bottom crust, cutting off the excess dough.
9. Brush pastry strips with cream and sprinkle with sugar.
10. Bake for about 40 minutes, or until dough is golden.
11. Remove from oven, let *crostata* cool slightly and remove the tart ring.
12. Serve with *gelato* or whipped cream. *Crostata* can be stored in the refrigerator for 3–4 days.

Suggested Pairing: Passito or Vin Santo

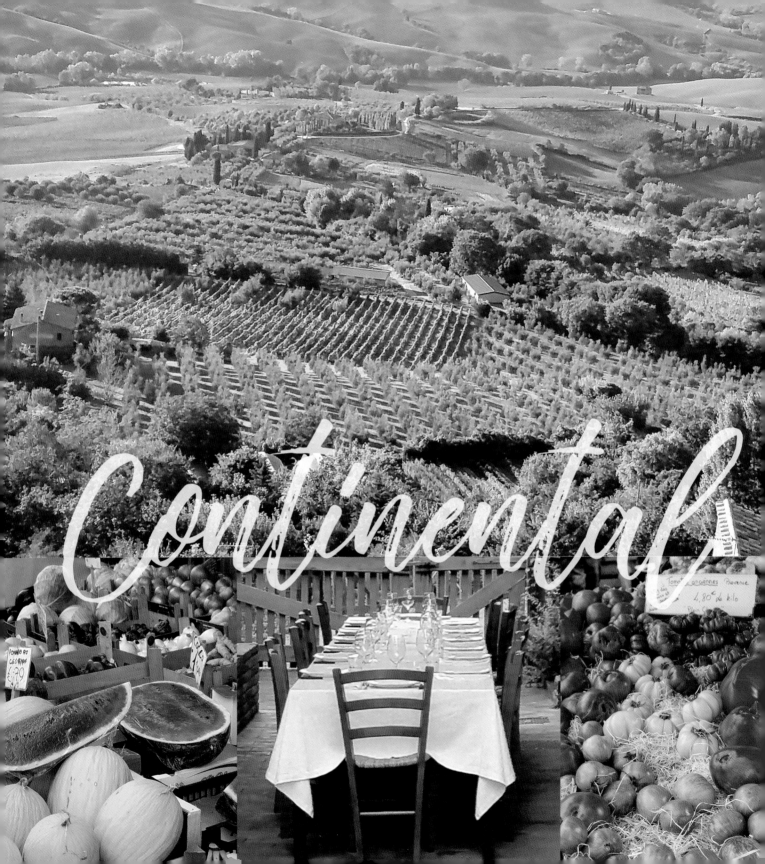

Continental

In continental Europe, brunch usually means a simple presentation of pastries, juice, and coffee. This menu, full of Mediterranean flavor, is a little more elaborate. With both sweet and savory dishes, it's a great choice for the holidays or a special wedding shower.

Brunch
ON THE CONTINENT

Comandante

Commander

Here's a cocktail that will make your taste buds stand up and salute! *Pamplemousse* or "grapefruit" sorbet with Champagne: a pairing that's so simple yet incredibly delicious. I first tasted it in Paris at Chez Margot, my favorite bistro in the *Marais arrondissement.* (I ordered this cocktail as an *aperitif* and enjoyed it so much that I had another for dessert!) Serve this gorgeous drink at a special brunch—or as a refreshing summer dessert or palette cleanser during an elegant multi-course meal.

Makes 8 cocktails

1 cup sugar
1 cup water
¼ cup grapefruit peel, finely diced
4 cups fresh ruby red grapefruit juice (5–6 grapefruits)
1 tablespoons fresh mint, finely chopped (optional)
1 bottle Champagne, Prosecco or other sparkling wine
Grapefruit wedges and fresh mint for garnish

1. Place sugar, water, and grapefruit peel in a small saucepan set over medium heat. Bring to a boil and simmer for 15 minutes. Set aside and cool to room temperature.
2. Pour syrup and peel into a large bowl, then add the grapefruit juice and mint (if using). Stir until evenly mixed. Cover and refrigerate until very cold (at least 2 hours) or overnight.
3. Transfer the mixture to an ice cream maker and freeze according to the manufacturer's instructions until sorbet is thick and slushy. Transfer the sorbet to a freezer-safe container, cover and freeze until firm before serving (3–4 hours). Sorbet can be frozen for up to 3 months.
4. When ready to serve, place a scoop of sorbet in martini or margarita glasses and pour Champagne over the top.
5. Garnish with grapefruit wedges and fresh mint sprigs. Serve with a *demitasse* spoon.

Notes

Other flavors of sorbet can be used to make this cocktail as well. If it is made with lemon sorbet, it is called a *"Colonel."* Mango or raspberry sorbets are also tasty choices.

Apricot Basil Preserves

Italian apricots are rosy, succulent, and make the best preserves. It's a popular filling for *cornetti* and jam *crostata*, or simply served with fresh butter and crusty bread. For this recipe, I elevated the apricots' soft sweetness with fresh basil and just a hint of red pepper. It's a jam worthy of Caesar himself!

Makes 1½ pints of preserves

1 pound fresh apricots
¼ cup freshly-squeezed lemon juice
1 cup sugar
1 cup loosely packed fresh basil leaves, finely chopped
½ teaspoon Michele Ferrante *Controne* Hot Pepper ♥

♥*See favorite products section on pages 170–176.*

1. Gently wash the apricots, cut them in half, and compost the pits.
2. Place apricot halves and lemon juice in the bowl of a food processor and pulse until puréed.
3. Remove the apricot purée and place in a heavy non-reactive saucepan set over medium heat. Add the sugar and basil leaves, then simmer for about 30 minutes, stirring from time to time, until thickened and jam coats the back of a spoon.
4. Stir in the red pepper flakes.
5. Transfer to sterilized jars, seal, and cool overnight. Preserves can be stored in the refrigerator for up to 1 month or frozen for up to 6 months.

Chorizo Potato Bake with Roasted Pepper Sauce

Sweet yet savory roasted pepper sauce and smoky Spanish *chorizo* make this recipe an outstanding choice for brunch. I like stacking the potato slices upright in a circle to create a dish as pretty as it is tasty. I make this in the 100-year-old cast iron skillet that I inherited from my dad—I know he would love it! You can also omit the *chorizo* for a delicious vegetarian option.

Serves 8

3 pounds Yellow Finn potatoes (about 6)
8 ounces smoked Spanish *chorizo*, sliced into chunks (see notes)
1½ cups Roasted Pepper Sauce (recipe on page 64)
1 cup chicken broth
Fresh thyme and rosemary for garnish

Notes

Smoked Spanish *chorizo* is cured, and different from raw Mexican *chorizo*. The Spanish style can be found at specialty food markets and online.

1. Preheat oven to 350°F.
2. Wash potatoes, but do not peel. Slice into ⅛-inch slices with a *mandoline* or sharp knife, and place in a large bowl.
3. Place the *chorizo* chunks in the bowl of a food processor and pulse several times until finely chopped. Add to the potatoes.
4. Pour the Roasted Pepper Sauce over the potato slices and *chorizo*. Mix together with hands until all the potato slices are coated with the sauce and the sausage is evenly distributed.
5. Arrange the potato slices standing upright in a round casserole dish or cast iron skillet. Pour the chicken broth over the potato mixture and bake for 1–1½ hours, or until the potatoes are golden and cooked through. Allow to rest for 5 minutes and sprinkle with fresh herbs before serving. This dish can be refrigerated for up to 1 week.

Pairing suggestion: Navarra red or rosé, Rioja, or Tempranillo

Cherry Tomato and Brie Clafoutis

Clafoutis is similar to a Dutch Baby. Traditionally made with cherries or other fruit, it's usually sweet. My savory version pairs fresh cherry tomatoes with thyme, *Brie*, and *Parmigiano-Reggiano* cheese. Enjoy this beautiful dish for a family brunch or light summer dinner—simply add a green salad.

Serves 8

2 tablespoons butter
12–14 cherry tomatoes, halved
3 eggs
⅓ cup whole milk
⅓ cup heavy cream
½ cup unbleached all-purpose flour
½ teaspoon sea salt
¼ teaspoon white pepper
2 teaspoons fresh thyme, minced
¼ cup *Parmigiano-Reggiano* cheese,
    plus 2 tablespoons, grated
2 ounces *Brie*, cut into small pieces

1. Preheat oven to 350°F.
2. Liberally butter a 10-inch round ceramic or glass baking dish (or a well-seasoned cast iron skillet). Place the tomatoes, cut-side down into the dish, distributing evenly.
3. In a large bowl, whisk together eggs, milk, and cream. Add flour, salt, white pepper, thyme, ¼ cup *Parmigiano-Reggiano* cheese, and whisk until just combined.
4. Pour the egg mixture on top of the tomatoes, redistributing tomatoes as needed.
5. Dot with *Brie* pieces and top with remaining *Parmigiano-Reggiano*. Bake until puffed and lightly browned (about 25–30 minutes).
6. Serve warm or at room temperature. *Clafoutis* is best served the day it is baked, but it can be stored in the refrigerator for 3–4 days.

Pairing suggestion: Sancerre rosé, Savignon Blanc, or sparkling wine

Cornetti

This Italian cousin of the French *croissant* is a little sweeter with a slightly softer texture. *Cornetti* can be made with butter or lard (yes, lard!), but the combination of the two creates a rich, buttery flavor and wonderfully fluffy texture. You can fill these flaky favorites with pastry cream, *Nutella*, or simply serve with jam—apricot being the most popular choice.

Makes 12 large cornetti

For the dough:
2 large eggs, lightly whisked
1½ cups of warm water
1 tablespoon plus ½ cup sugar, divided
5½–6 cups "00" ♥ or unbleached
    all-purpose flour, divided
2¼ teaspoons instant yeast
2 tablespoons unsalted butter, melted
1 teaspoon vanilla extract
2 tablespoons orange zest
½ cup nonfat dry milk powder
1 tablespoon fine sea salt

For the butter:
1 cup unsalted butter, room temp.
1 cup lard (see notes on page 56)
¾ teaspoon salt
½ cup "00" ♥ or unbleached
    all-purpose flour

For the glaze:
1 egg
1 tablespoon water
Pearl sugar, optional

♥See favorite products section on pages 170–176.

Notes

Lard can be found in the baking section of most grocery stores. I prefer Morrell Snowcap or Armour brands.

For the dough:
1. Create a "sponge" by placing the eggs and water in a large mixing bowl. Add 1 tablespoon of the sugar, 3 cups of flour, and the yeast. Mix until well blended; set aside for 15–20 minutes until the sponge begins to bubble.

For the butter:
2. Cut the butter and lard into 1-inch chunks and place in the bowl of a stand mixer fitted with a paddle attachment. Add the salt and the flour and mix at low speed until just smooth, with no visible lumps.
3. Spread the butter/lard mixture on a piece of plastic wrap and shape into an 8-inch square. Wrap and refrigerate for at least 1 hour.

Finish the dough:
4. Add the melted butter, vanilla, and orange zest to the sponge. Whisk together and add remaining ½ cup sugar, 2½ cups of the flour, the dry milk, and salt. Mix until the dough forms. Tip dough onto a lightly-floured surface and knead for 5–10 minutes. If the dough is sticky to the touch, add the remaining flour 2 tablespoons at a time until the dough reaches the desired consistency. It should be smooth and elastic but not stick to your fingers. Pat the dough into a 9-inch square, wrap in plastic and refrigerate for 1 hour.

To laminate the dough:
5. Remove the chilled dough from the refrigerator and gently roll it into a 12-inch square.
6. Unwrap the butter square and place in the center of the dough at a 45° angle, so it looks like a diamond inside a square. Pull the corners of the dough into the center of the butter. Pinch the seams together to enclose the butter. Dust the top with flour and turn the dough over.
7. Tap the dough all over with a rolling pin, encouraging it into an even rectangular shape. Roll into a 20 x 10-inch rectangle, picking it up and dusting lightly with flour as needed.

Recipe continues on next page.

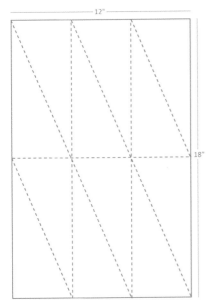

fig. 1

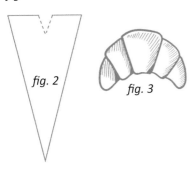

fig. 2

fig. 3

8. When the dough has reached the proper size, dust off any excess flour and fold it into thirds, like a business letter. Take care to keep the edges straight. Wrap the dough in plastic and refrigerate for 1 hour to allow the gluten in the dough to relax.

9. Repeat steps 7 and 8 two more times, refrigerating for 1 hour in between rolling and folding.

10. Refrigerate the dough overnight before using. You can also freeze the dough for up to 3 months at this point.

Shape the cornetti:

11. Line 2 baking sheets with parchment paper or silicone baking mats.

12 Roll the dough into a 13 x 19-inch rectangle. Using a pizza wheel or a sharp knife, trim the edges ½ inch all the way around (even up the edges to make a 12 x 18-inch rectangle). This removes the folded edges that would inhibit the dough's rise.

13. Cut the dough in thirds lengthwise and in half down the center. This will give you six 4 x 9-inch pieces. Cut these pieces in half diagonally (see fig. 1). Arrange dough triangles so the tips are facing toward you and stretch them gently to make them a little longer (gently tacking the tip to the work surface helps keep it in place), then cut a 1-inch notch in the center of the wide end of each triangle (see fig. 2).

14. Take the 2 inside corners of the notched wide end and roll them toward you, building a curved shape as you roll the dough toward the tip. Make sure the tip ends under the bottom of the *cornetto* (see fig. 3). Place the shaped pastry on prepared baking sheets (6 per sheet). Cover them with a tea towel and let rise for about 90 minutes. *Cornetti* will visibly rise, but not double in size.

15. Preheat the oven to 425°F. Brush each *cornetto* with an egg beaten with 1 tablespoon water, then sprinkle with pearl sugar (optional). Bake for 15 minutes, then reduce the temperature to 350°F and bake for 10–15 minutes more, until deep golden brown and no raw dough is visible where layers overlap. Remove from the oven, place baking pan on a cooling rack, and cool 15–20 minutes before serving.

16. Serve with butter and Apricot Basil Preserves (recipe on page 49).

European Greens and Berries with Limoncello Dressing

If you're looking for a salad that's as gorgeous as it is delicious, here you go. This recipe works wonderfully for a brunch buffet or as the starter for an elegant supper. The *limoncello* and mint dressing highlights the garden-fresh flavor, and the mixed berries make it picture-perfect.

Serves 8

For the salad:
4 cups European greens such as arugula, endive, and *radicchio*
2 cups mixed fresh berries

For the dressing:
3 tablespoons Ritrovo Selections Citrus Balsamic Vinegar ♥
1 tablespoon *limoncello* liqueur
⅓ cup extra virgin olive oil
2 tablespoons fresh mint, minced
Sea salt & freshly ground black pepper
Mint and edible flowers for garnish

♥*See favorite products section on pages 170–176.*

For the salad:
1. Place greens and berries in a large serving bowl and gently mix.

For the dressing:
2. Whisk together the Citrus Balsamic Vinegar and *limoncello,* and slowly drizzle in the extra virgin olive oil, whisking to incorporate. Add the fresh mint, and season with sea salt and freshly ground pepper to taste.
3. Pour the dressing over the salad and toss. Serve with additional mint and edible flowers.

Pairing suggestion: Fruity rosato or Prosecco

Aperol Olive Oil Pound Cake

Yogurt and olive oil give this cake a wonderfully moist texture while the Aperol adds a surprising herbaceous flavor. A tasty dessert, it's also an ideal choice for a brunch menu—especially when served with a vibrant Aperol Spritz!

For the cake:
1½ cups unbleached all-purpose flour
2 teaspoons baking powder
½ teaspoon sea salt
1 cup plain whole-milk yogurt
1 cup sugar
3 extra-large eggs
2 teaspoons lemon zest, grated
1 teaspoon vanilla extract
2 tablespoons Aperol (see notes)
½ cup Casina Rossa Extra Virgin Olive Oil with Sicilian Lemon ♥

For the glaze:
1 cup confectioners' sugar
2 teaspoons freshly squeezed lemon or orange juice
2 tablespoons Aperol
Orange zest

♥*See favorite products on pages 170–176.*

Notes

Aperol is an Italian bitter orange *aperitif.* Other orange liqueur or *limoncello* can be substituted. See page 12 for more options.

For the cake:
1. Preheat oven to 350°F. Butter a 1-pound loaf pan and line with parchment paper.
2. Sift together the flour, baking powder, and salt into a large mixing bowl and set aside.
3. Place the yogurt, sugar, eggs, lemon zest, vanilla extract, and Aperol in a small mixing bowl; whisk until smooth and well combined.
4. Slowly whisk the flour mixture into the wet ingredients until smooth. With a rubber spatula, fold the olive oil into the batter, making sure it's completely incorporated.
5. Pour the batter into the prepared pan and bake for about 50 minutes, or until a cake tester placed in the center of the loaf comes out clean.
6. Allow the cake to cool for 5–10 minutes and remove to a cooling rack.

For the glaze:
7. Place the confectioners' sugar and the lemon or orange juice in a small bowl. Add the Aperol and mix well. Drizzle glaze over the warm cake, sprinkle with orange zest, and allow the cake to cool.
8. Serve with whipped cream or Shortcut "Clotted Cream" (recipe on page 108). Cake can be refrigerated for up to 1 week or frozen for up to 3 months.

Pairing suggestion: Aperol Spritz (recipe on page 12)

Collioure

A picturesque fishing village on the southeastern coast of France, Collioure attracts tourists and artists from all over the world. The narrow streets and cobblestone alleys are lined with charming shops, color-filled galleries, and tapas bars that serve small plates of local specialties. Collioure's cuisine is heavily influenced by neighboring Catalonia in Spain; I have adapted a sampling of my favorite dishes for this menu.

Catalan Cuisine
IN COLLIOURE

Sparkling Saffron Sangria

Saffron-infused vodka is the secret to this sangria's lovely golden color and surprising zest—which perfectly complements this Catalan menu. Fill each glass with fresh fruit and berries for a glorious presentation of color and flavor.

Makes 4–6 cocktails

1 bottle Cava (see notes)
¼ cup Saffron-Infused Vodka (recipe below)
¾ cup Cointreau
¼ cup orange juice, freshly squeezed
3 cups fresh berries, divided
2 oranges (plus more for garnish), sliced
1 tablespoon fresh mint, minced

1. Pour Cava into a pitcher; add vodka, Cointreau, and orange juice.
2. Add 2 cups of the mixed berries, sliced oranges, and mint. Refrigerate for 1–2 hours before serving.
3. Thread remaining berries onto cocktail skewers.
4. When ready to serve, pour sangria into goblets, spoon in fruit, and garnish with an orange slice and berry skewer.

Saffron-Infused Vodka

2 cups vodka
1 large pinch saffron threads

1. Place the vodka and saffron threads in a sterilized bottle. Store in a cool, dark place for 1 week, shaking occasionally. Use to garnish soups or make unique cocktails. Saffron vodka will keep in the freezer indefinitely.

Notes

Cava is a sparkling wine from Spain. It may be *blanco* (white) or *rosado* (rosé).

The Spanish Cava label is similar to the Champagne designation in France in that only wines produced by the traditional method may be sold as Cava. Wines produced by any other method can only be called "sparkling wines." Most Cava is made in the Penedès area in Catalonia in northeastern Spain.

Champagne, *Prosecco*, or other sparkling wine can be used for this *sangria* as well.

Almonds and Olives

Here's an easy appetizer with a burst of tastes and textures. Warming the olives with nuts, rosemary, and lemon zest mellows and blends the flavors perfectly. Serve over a scoop of *Romesco* Sauce (recipe on page 65) for a unique and deliciously healthy snack.

Makes 3 cups

2–3 tablespoons extra virgin olive oil
5–6 garlic cloves, roughly chopped
2 tablespoons fresh rosemary leaves
1 cup almonds, roasted and salted
1 cup *Castelvetrano* olives
1 cup dry-cured black olives
Zest of 1 lemon
Michele Ferrante *Controne* Hot Pepper ♥ (optional)

♥*See favorite products section on pages 170–176.*

1. Place oil in small heavy-bottom skillet set over medium heat.
2. Add garlic and reduce heat to medium low, stirring occasionally until golden and fragrant.
3. Add rosemary leaves and stir 1–2 minutes until fragrant.
4. Add nuts and olives and sauté, stirring occasionally until both are warm (about 5–7 minutes).
5. Stir in the lemon zest and red paper flakes. Serve this dish warm on its own or on top of a scoop of *Romesco* Sauce (recipe on page 65). The mixture can be stored in the refrigerator for up to 10 days and reheated before serving.

Pairing suggestion: Albariño, Vinoh Verde, or a dry Sherry such as Fino or Manzanilla

Notes

Any combination of nuts and olives can be used in this simple appetizer.

It is nice to combine brine-cured and dry-cured olives. Brine-cured olives are soaked in salt water for 3–12 months. Dry-cured olives are packed in salt for a month or longer, then rinsed and usually stored in olive oil.

Castelvetrano olives are my favorite brine-cured olives because of their mild flavor and firm texture. They also pair well with more pungent varieties such as *Kalamata* and *Nyon*.

Bûcheron with Roasted Pepper Sauce

Roasting peppers gives them a mild, sweet flavor and adds smoky deliciousness. Enjoy this savory sauce as a condiment with fish, pasta, and poultry. I especially love the flavor it adds to my *Chorizo* Potato Bake (recipe on page 50).

Makes about 1½ cups

4 red bell peppers (or a 15-ounce jar of roasted red peppers)
3 garlic cloves, roughly chopped
1 tablespoon fresh thyme leaves, minced
1 tablespoon fresh rosemary, minced
1 tablespoon Ritrovo Selections Organic Tomato Balsamic Vinegar ♥
1 teaspoon Fior di Maiella Smoked Sweet Pepper Powder ♥
½ teaspoon Michele Ferrante *Controne* Hot Pepper ♥
½ teaspoon sea salt
¼ cup extra virgin olive oil
2 ounces *Bûcheron* goat cheese (see notes)
Extra virgin olive oil and fresh rosemary for garnish

♥*See favorite products section on pages 170–176.*

1. Preheat oven to 400°F and line a baking sheet with aluminum foil.
2. Place peppers on the baking sheet and roast for 20–30 minutes, turning from time to time until the skins have blackened.
3. Place the hot peppers in a large paper bag and fold top over to seal, and allow to cool (about 10–15 minutes). Then peel off the skins, core and de-seed them. (If using preserved peppers, skip the first 3 steps.)
4. Place the peppers, garlic, thyme, rosemary, tomato balsamic, smoked pepper powder, red pepper flakes, and salt in the bowl of a food processor. Blend to a puree.
5. With the motor running, gradually pour in the extra virgin olive oil. Taste for seasoning and add more sea salt and red pepper flakes to taste. Sauce can be stored in the refrigerator for 7–10 days.
6. When ready to serve, preheat oven to 350°F and remove the *Bûcheron* from the refrigerator.
7. Place about 1 cup of the sauce in a small baking dish, position the round of *Bûcheron* in the center, and bake until the cheese is slightly melted and the sauce is bubbling (10–15 minutes). Drizzle with extra virgin olive oil and garnish with fresh rosemary.

Pairing suggestion: Rioja or Tempranillo

Notes

Bûcheron is a goat cheese from Loire Valley in central France. It offers the taste and texture of two cheeses in one. This cheese usually ripens for 5–10 weeks, resulting in a dense center surrounded by a gooey creamy line of rich flavor encased in an edible bloomy rind.

Bûcheron is the perfect choice for this appetizer, but other soft-ripened goat cheeses can be used as well.

Romesco Sauce

Both healthy and delicious, this *Romesco* Sauce is without a doubt my favorite condiment. It pairs beautifully with everything—a piece of chicken, pork, beef, or seafood. I also think it's divine simply spread on crusty bread.

Makes about 2 cups

1 cup almonds, raw, slivered
1 head of garlic, top ¼ sliced off
2 large tomatoes
3 medium red and orange bell peppers (see notes)
2 tablespoons Ritrovo Selections Tomato Balsamic Vinegar ♥
1 tablespoon Fior di Maiella Smoked Sweet Pepper Powder ♥
1 teaspoon Ritrovo Selections Saffron&Salt ♥
¼ cup extra virgin olive oil
⅛ teaspoon Michele Ferrante *Controne* Hot Pepper ♥

♥*See favorite products section on pages 170–176.*

1. Preheat oven to 375°F. Line a baking pan with aluminum foil. Place almonds, garlic (top side down), and tomatoes on the baking sheet; then roast until almonds are fragrant and just starting to brown, (10–15 minutes). Remove almonds and continue to roast garlic until soft and tomatoes until tender (about 20 minutes more). Remove from oven, let cool slightly and remove skin from tomatoes, peel garlic, and set aside.
2. While other ingredients are in the oven, roast peppers over an open flame on a gas stove or grill until the skins are blackened (they can also be broiled in the oven). Place peppers in a paper bag, fold top over to seal and let cool. Peel off skin, core and de-seed.
3. Place almonds in the bowl of a food processor and pulse until finely chopped. Add peppers, tomatoes, garlic, vinegar, smoked pepper powder, and salt. Pulse until well combined. Slowly drizzle in the olive oil and process until smooth. Add salt and hot pepper flakes as desired.
4. Serve warm or at room temperature. Store in an airtight container in the refrigerator up to 5 days or in the freezer for 3 months.

Notes

Any combination of red and orange bell peppers can be used. I prefer to mix them because I love the deep orange color it creates in the sauce.

Chicken Skewers with Romesco Sauce

This recipe is a great addition to any tapas party menu: tender chicken thighs marinated in smoked pepper, garlic, tomato balsamic, and olive oil, served with savory *Romesco* Sauce. It makes a light and healthy entrée for a summer meal on the deck—just add a green salad and you're done.

Serves 4–6

**2 pounds chicken thighs, trimmed
    and cut into 2-inch chunks**
¼ cup extra virgin olive oil
¼ cup fresh parsley, minced
1 tablespoon fresh oregano, minced
4 garlic cloves, minced
**4 teaspoons Fior di Maiella Smoked
    Sweet Pepper Powder ♥**
**2 tablespoons Ritrovo Selections
    Organic Tomato Balsamic
    Vinegar ♥**
**2 teaspoons Casina Rossa
    Herbs&Salt ♥**
**Michele Ferrante *Controne*
    Hot Pepper ♥**
***Romesco* Sauce (recipe on page 65)**

*♥See favorite products section
on pages 170–176.*

1. Place the chicken pieces in a glass bowl.
2. Place the remaining ingredients in a small bowl and whisk together until emulsified; pour over the chicken. Mix to coat all the chicken pieces with the marinade and refrigerate for at least 4 hours (or overnight for best flavor).
3. Thread chicken pieces onto barbecue skewers. If using wooden skewers, be sure to soak in water for at least 30 minutes before threading on the chicken so skewers won't burn on the grill.
4. Grill the chicken skewers on a barbecue over medium heat for about 15–20 minutes until cooked through and browned, turning a quarter turn every 3–4 minutes to make sure the chicken doesn't burn.
5. Serve with *Romesco* Sauce (recipe on page 65). Chicken can be stored in the refrigerator for 4–5 days.

Pairing suggestion: Cava, Rioja, or rosado

Pickled Red Onions

I love pickling red onions because it tames their burn and sweetens their flavor. These pretty pink slices are delicious in salads, as well as on burgers and other sandwiches.

Makes about 1 pint

1 bay leaf
2 garlic cloves, halved
½ teaspoon peppercorns
1 tablespoon sugar
1 tablespoon sea salt
1 small large red onion, halved and sliced thinly
1 cup Ritrovo Selections White Balsamic Vinegar ♥
1 cup boiling water (more or less)

♥ *See favorite products section on pages 170–176.*

1. Place bay leaf, garlic, peppercorns, sugar, and sea salt in the bottom of a sterilized 1-pint jar. Pack in the sliced onions, leaving about ½ inch to the top of jar. Pour in the vinegar.
2. Add boiling water to the jar (enough to cover onion slices), cover, and shake well. Refrigerate for at least 30 minutes; overnight for best flavor. Pickled onions will keep in the refrigerator for 2–3 weeks.

Roasted Brussels Sprout Salad

Brussels sprouts and bacon are a match made in heaven. The addition of pickled onions and blood orange adds a brightness in flavor and color. Serve this unique salad warm or at room temperature.

Serves 6

For the salad:
½ cup smoked bacon, slivered
1 pound Brussels sprouts, halved
2 tablespoons extra virgin olive oil
½ cup water
1 blood orange, peeled, quartered
　　and cut into ¼-inch slices
½ cup pickled red onion slices
　　(recipe on opposite page)
¼ cup pine nuts, toasted
½ cup *Manchego* cheese, shaved

For the dressing:
2 tablespoons Ritrovo Selections
　　Citrus Balsamic Vinegar ♥
1 garlic clove, minced
½ teaspoon sea salt
¼ cup olive oil
Freshly ground black pepper

♥*See favorite products section on pages 170–176.*

For the salad :
1. Place bacon in a large skillet set over medium high heat and sauté until browned and crispy. Set aside, reserving the oil in the pan. Add olive oil.
2. Place the Brussels sprouts, cut side down, in the hot oil and cook for 2–3 minutes until browned. Stir the sprouts and cook for an additional 2–3 minutes.
3. Add the water and cover the skillet to allow the sprouts to steam until tender (3–4 minutes; do not overcook). Transfer to a serving bowl and, while the Brussels sprouts are still hot, add the bacon, orange slices, pickled red onions, and pine nuts. Stir to combine and allow to cool to room temperature.

For the dressing:
4. Place the citrus balsamic, garlic, and sea salt in a small bowl and whisk together. Drizzle in the olive oil, a little at a time, while whisking. Add additional sea salt and freshly ground pepper to taste.
5. Just before serving, gently stir in the shaved *Manchego* cheese. Serve slightly warm or at room temperature. Salad will keep in the refrigerator for up to 5 days. Bring up to room temperature before serving.

Pairing suggestion: Rosado or Cava

Zarzuela de Mariscos

Catalan Seafood Stew

Zarzuela is a rich shellfish stew similar to *bouillabaisse* and *cioppino*, but enhanced with red peppers and almonds—both staples in Catalonian cuisine. I add *Romesco* Sauce for an even greater depth of flavor.

Serves 6–8

1 pound medium shrimp with shells
1 pound Manila clams
1 pound mussels
½ cup dry white wine
Large pinch of saffron
2 cups clam juice
2 cups vegetable (or chicken) stock
2 bay leaves
4 ounces *Iberico* ham or
    prosciutto, diced
¼ cup extra virgin olive oil
1 large onion, diced
1 red bell pepper, diced
1–2 teaspoons sea salt
5 garlic cloves, minced
1 tablespoon fresh rosemary, minced
1 tablespoon fresh oregano, minced
1 tablespoon fresh thyme leaves
1 cup tomatoes, diced
½ teaspoon Michele Ferrante
    Controne Hot Pepper ♥
1 cup *Romesco* Sauce
    (recipe on page 65)
Juice of 1 lemon
¼ cup fresh flat leaf parsley, chopped
1 lemon, cut into 8 wedges
Fior di Maiella Smoked Sweet
    Pepper Powder ♥

♥ *See favorite products section on pages 170–176.*

1. Peel the shrimp, reserving the shells for the stock. Rinse the clams in cold water, then scrub and de-beard the mussels. Set aside in the refrigerator.
3. Pour the white wine into a small bowl, add the saffron, and allow to "bloom."
4. Pour the clam juice and vegetable stock into a stock pot set over low heat. Add the shrimp shells and bay leaves. Leave stock to simmer, covered, as you prepare the rest of the dish.
5. Set a heavy skillet or Dutch oven over medium-high heat, add the *prosciutto and* sauté to brown slightly and render some of the fat. Remove from skillet and set aside.
6. Reduce the heat to medium and add olive oil, onion, peppers, and sea salt. Sauté until the vegetables start to become tender (about 8 minutes).
7. Add the garlic, rosemary, oregano, and thyme. Continue to sauté until the garlic is cooked (about 5 minutes).
8. Add the wine to deglaze the pan for few minutes, then add tomatoes and the red pepper flakes. Pour in most of the stock, making sure there is room in the pan for the shellfish. Bring to a boil and allow to simmer for about 5 minutes.
9. Add the *Romesco* Sauce; stir to incorporate it into the soup.
10. Add the shrimp, mussels, and clams. Continue to simmer until shrimp are pink and cooked through and mussels and clams open up (it will only take a few minutes). Discard any clams or mussels that do not open.
11. Remove from heat and squeeze in the juice of 1 lemon. Season to taste with additional salt and red pepper flakes.
12. Place in shallow bowls and garnish with parsley and lemon wedges dipped in Smoked Sweet Pepper Powder. *Zarzuela* will keep in the refrigerator for 3–4 days.

Pairing suggestion: Spanish white such as Albarino or Godella, a red such as Garnacha, or a well-aged Rioja

Tarta de Almendras

Almond Tart

The ideal end to our tapas party, this tart layers almonds with a surprising burst of orange and cinnamon. The crust does not require blind baking (see notes), but it's important to bake long enough to ensure that the bottom crust is brown and crispy. I like to serve this tart with vanilla bean ice cream or whipped cream for a real treat.

*Makes one 11-inch tart
or six 4-inch tarts*

For the pastry:
1¾ cup unbleached all-purpose flour
⅔ cup sugar
½ teaspoon sea salt
½ cup cold unsalted butter, cut
    into ½-inch cubes
1 egg
1–2 tablespoons iced water

For the filling:
4 eggs
2 cups sugar
Zest of 1 orange
1 teaspoon almond extract
2 cups almond meal
1 pinch ground cinnamon
1 cup almonds, slivered
Confectioners' sugar

Notes

Blind baking is a method in which the raw pastry crust is fitted into the pan, lined with foil, filled with baking beans or pie weights, and pre-baked before adding the filling.

For the pastry:
1. Place flour, sugar, and salt in the bowl of a food processor and pulse until just combined. Add the butter, 1 cube at a time, and pulse until mixture resembles coarse bread crumbs. Add egg, pulse to incorporate, then add cold water, 1 tablespoon at a time. Pulse until pastry just comes together. Form pastry into a flat disc, wrap in plastic, and refrigerate for 30 minutes.

For the filling:
2. Place eggs and sugar in a large bowl; whisk until the mixture is pale, frothy, and has doubled in size. Fold in orange zest, almond extract, almond meal, and cinnamon.
3. Preheat oven to 350°F. Roll out pastry on a lightly floured work surface into about an 11-inch circle that is ⅛-inch thick. Line removable bottom tart tin with pastry; press in, and trim edges. Prick base with a fork. (If using 4-inch tart tins, divide the dough into 6 portions and roll each into ⅛-inch thick circle.)
4. Spoon almond filling into tart tin and smooth top with an offset spatula and sprinkle with slivered almonds.
5. Bake for 50 minutes or until golden. To prevent top from burning, cover with foil the last 10 minutes of baking. (If using 4-inch tart tins, they will require less baking time.)
6. Cool tart in pan, then remove and serve at room temperature dusted with confectioners' sugar. Tart will keep in the refrigerator for up to 5 days. It is also delicious for breakfast with a *cappuccino*.

Pairing suggestion: Cream or Oloroso Sherry

Carcassonne

Located in the Aude region of southern France, Carcassonne is an ancient citadel city. Along with Toulouse and Castelnaudary, Carcassonne claims to have created the original recipe for *Cassoulet*. The ultimate French comfort food, *Cassoulet* is a decadent classic and perfect for your next dinner party—regardless of its exact origin.

Cassoulet IN CARCASSONNE

La Dame Blanche

The White Lady of Carcassonne haunts the taste buds. Don't let the egg whites scare you: they add a distinctive ghostly color—and protein! You won't taste them either.

Makes 1 cocktail

1 egg white (or 2 tablespoons pasteurized egg whites)
2 ounces gin
¾ ounce *Cointreau*
½ ounce fresh lemon juice
Lemon twist for garnish

1. Pour egg white, gin, *Cointreau*, and lemon juice into a cocktail shaker without ice, and shake vigorously.
2. Add ice and shake again until well chilled.
3. Strain into a *coupe* cocktail glass. Garnish with the lemon twist.

Crème Fraîche

Makes 2 cups

2 cups heavy cream (40% or more butterfat content)
1 tablespoon cultured buttermilk, or plain yogurt

1. Heat the cream in a non-reactive pot to 72°F.
2. Add the cultured buttermilk or yogurt and stir.
3. Place in an airtight jar and leave out at room temperature until the *crème fraîche* thickens, 24–48 hours. Once it's thickened, place in the refrigerator to stop the cultures from growing. It will keep in the refrigerator for up to 2 weeks.

Smoked Salmon Rillettes

Rillettes by any other name is just a spread. Although it sounds elegant and tastes incredible, this lovely appetizer is surprisingly easy to prepare. The secret is to purchase good quality smoked salmon.

Makes about 2 cups

¼ cup pickled red onion, finely chopped (recipe on page 68)
1 cup *crème fraîche* (recipe on opposite page)
½ cup unsalted butter, softened
8 ounces smoked salmon
1 tablespoon capers
Zest and juice of 1 lemon
½ teaspoon sea salt
½ teaspoon white pepper
¼ cup finely chopped chives, plus more for garnish
Baguette slices for serving (recipe on page 141)

1. Place pickled onions, *crème fraîche,* and butter in the bowl of a food processor and pulse until smooth. Add salmon and capers; process until salmon is coarsely chopped and incorporated (about 15–20 seconds).
2. Transfer mixture to a medium bowl and stir in lemon zest, lemon juice, sea salt, white pepper, and chives. Season to taste.
3. Spread *rillettes* on *baguette* slices, and top with chives and sea salt. *Rillettes* will keep in the refrigerator for 2–3 days,

Pairing suggestion: Champagne or other sparkling wine

Frisée with Lardon and Walnuts

This classic salad is simple, delicious and the perfect light start for a heavy meal. The walnut vinegar is unusual, and paired with walnut oil and walnuts, it offers mouth-watering layers of flavor.

Serves 8

For the salad:
4 ounces *lardon* (unsmoked bacon), or thick bacon, cut into ¼-inch strips
1 large head *frisée*, torn into bite-sized pieces
½ cup walnuts, coarsely chopped and toasted
½ cup aged *Gruyère* cheese, shaved

For the dressing:
2 tablespoons Edmund Fallot Walnut Vinegar ♥
4 tablespoons walnut oil
Sea salt & freshly ground black pepper

♥*See favorite products section on pages 170–176.*

1. Set a small skillet over medium heat, add the *lardon* or bacon, and cook until crispy. Set aside to drain on paper towel, reserving the oil in the pan. Allow the oil to cool slightly.
2. Add the vinegar to the reserved oil and whisk to combine. Slowly drizzle in the walnut oil, whisking continually. Season with salt and black pepper.
3. Place *frisée* in a large serving bowl, add *lardon* or bacon, walnuts, and dressing; toss well. Sprinkle with shaved *Gruyère* and more black pepper if desired.

Suggested pairing: Chardonnay or sparkling white

Vegetable Tian

A *tian* is a traditional French pottery vessel used both for cooking and serving. It is also the name of this classic recipe for colorful vegetables stacked with herbs and olive oil. Healthy and fresh, it makes a delicious side or vegetarian entrée. If you don't have a ceramic *tian*, bake the vegetables in a pretty casserole dish—it goes from oven to table with ease.

Serves 8

3 tablespoons extra virgin olive oil, plus more for oiling pan
1 tablespoon Ritrovo Selections Organic Tomato Balsamic Vinegar ♥
3 garlic cloves, minced
1 tablespoon fresh thyme leaves, plus extra sprigs for top
1 teaspoon sea salt
½ teaspoon freshly ground black pepper
1 pound green zucchini
1 pound yellow zucchini
1 pound eggplant
4 medium tomatoes
½ cup *Parmigiano-Reggiano* cheese, grated

♥ *See favorite products section on pages 170–176.*

1. Preheat the oven to 350°F.
2. Brush a round 10-inch baking dish with extra virgin olive oil.
3. Place extra virgin olive oil, Tomato Balsamic Vinegar, garlic, thyme, sea salt, and freshly ground pepper in a large bowl; whisk until well combined.
4. Using a *mandoline* or sharp knife, cut the zucchini, eggplant, and tomatoes into ¼-inch-thick slices. Place vegetables in the bowl with the olive oil mixture and, using hands, mix together and cover each slice with the dressing.
5. Arrange vegetables on end in the baking dish, alternating zucchini, eggplant, and tomatoes, fitting them tightly in a circle around the dish and then filling the middle. Drizzle vegetables with 1 more tablespoon of extra virgin olive oil and top with a few thyme sprigs. Cover the dish with a lid or aluminum foil.
6. Bake for 30 minutes, then uncover the dish, remove the thyme sprigs, and sprinkle with the *Parmigiano-Reggiano* cheese. Bake for another 40 minutes, or until vegetables are tender and browned on top.
7. Serve warm or at room temperature. Store in the refrigerator for 3–5 days. Use leftover veggies with *Romesco* Sauce (recipe on page 65) and fresh *mozzarella* for great grilled *panini*.

Suggested pairing: Bordeaux rosé

Cassoulet

A rich combination of white beans, duck or goose *confit*, sausages, and pork, *cassoulet* cooks slowly in the oven in a ceramic or cast iron pot. It takes all day to prepare, but—I think you'll agree—it's well worth the effort.

Serves 4-6

For the cassoulet:
1 pound dried *Flageolet* or *cannellini* beans, soaked overnight in 3 times their volume of water
1 cup bacon, cut into ¼-inch strips
1 ham hock
2 tablespoons extra virgin olive oil
1 stalk celery, roughly chopped
1 onion, roughly chopped
2 large carrots, roughly chopped
6 garlic cloves, roughly chopped
2 ripe plum tomatoes, diced
2 bay leaves
4 sprigs thyme
4 sprigs parsley
2 teaspoons sea salt
1 teaspoon freshly ground black pepper
4 garlic sausages
1 tablespoon lemon juice
4 legs duck *confit* (see notes)

For the bread crumb topping:
2 tablespoons extra virgin olive oil
1 cup dried bread crumbs
1 garlic clove, minced
¼ cup Italian parsley, coarsely chopped

1. Drain the soaked beans and discard the soaking water. Pour the beans into a large Dutch oven or soup pot, add the bacon and ham hock and cover with fresh cold water. Set heat to medium, bring to a boil, and simmer for about 30 minutes.
2. Preheat the oven to 250°F.
3. Heat the olive oil in a heavy skillet set over low heat. Add the celery, onion, carrots, and garlic; sauté for a few minutes, cover and allow to sweat for another 5 minutes. Add the tomatoes and herbs; cook until caramelized (about 5 minutes). Add the vegetables to the beans and gently stir to combine.
4. Set the skillet over medium-high heat and brown the sausages on all sides. Add them to the beans.
5. Place Dutch oven (or transfer to a large casserole dish) and set on the middle rack of oven. Cook, uncovered, for 2 hours, stirring every hour. At the end of this time, the beans will be soft and creamy in texture and the juices should have thickened. It may take longer to get to this stage, depending on the beans used.
6. Remove the *cassoulet* from the oven. Transfer the ham hock to a cutting surface and, using a fork, remove the meat and add it back to the *cassoulet*, discarding the bone. Squeeze the lemon juice over the beans and stir to combine. Bury the duck legs in the beans.

Finish with bread crumb topping:
7. Combine olive oil, bread crumbs, and minced garlic; sprinkle over the cassoulet. Return to the oven and cook for an additional 2 hours more, until most of the liquid has been absorbed and the bread crumb topping is nicely browned.
8. Serve the cassoulet in bowls, sprinkled with chopped parsley if desired. Cassoulet is great the second day and will keep in the refrigerator for 4–5 days. It can also be frozen for up to 3 months.

Pairing suggestion: Côte du Rhone red or rosé

Notes

Duck *confit* is made by braising salted duck legs in fat. It can be found in specialty food markets and online.

Tarte au Citron

Lemon Tart

This no-bake lemon tart is a showpiece piled high with fresh berries and decorated with mint. The cookie crust makes it easy—it's easier still if you use store-bought lemon curd.

Serves 8

For the crust:
Shortbread cookies, such as *Lorna Doone* (enough to make 1½ cups cookie crumbs)
½ cup almond meal
6 tablespoons butter, melted

For the filling:
1 cup heavy whipping cream
4 ounces cream cheese, softened
8 ounces *mascarpone* cheese, at room temperature
¼ cup confectioners' sugar
¾ cup lemon curd (recipe on page 113, or use store-bought)
2 teaspoons lemon zest
Fresh berries and mint for garnish

For the crust:
1. Place the cookies in the large bowl of a food processor and pulse until finely crumbled.
2. Measure 1½ cups of cookie crumbs and place them in a large bowl. Add the almond meal and whisk until thoroughly combined. Drizzle the melted butter over the crumbs, and stir or mix with fingers until thoroughly combined.
3. Turn the crumb mixture out into a 10-inch tart pan (square or round). Press down and into the edges until firmly packed and uniform.
4. Place in the freezer for 15–20 minutes, or refrigerate until solid.

For the filling:
5. Place the heavy whipping cream and cream cheese in the large bowl of a stand mixer fitted with a whisk attachment. Beat until smooth and silky, about 3 minutes on high speed.
6. Add the *mascarpone* and confectioners' sugar; beat on low until just combined (overbeating will cause the *mascarpone* to separate).
7. Fold in the lemon curd and lemon zest until combined, then pour into prepared tart shell and smooth with an offset spatula.
8. Cover and refrigerate for a minimum of 3 hours. Garnish with mixed berries and mint. Tart can be stored in the refrigerator for 3–5 days.

Suggested pairing: Limoncello liqueur or a sweet sparkling wine

Paris

Because Paris is *always* a good idea—and so are cocktails! Dress up in your finest fashions, slip into your *Louboutins* (If you're lucky enough to own a pair!), watch *Sabrina*, and enjoy this elegant Parisian-themed cocktail party with your *amis. A votre santé!*

Cocktails
IN PARIS

Bubbles in the Louvre

Mona Lisa's smile has just turned into a grin—thanks to this lovely Champagne cocktail.

Makes 1 cocktail

1 ounce St. Germain Elderflower Liqueur
1 ounce Grey Goose Vodka
½ ounce lemon juice, freshly squeezed
½ ounce simple syrup (recipe on page 15)
Pink Champagne or other sparkling rosé wine
Raspberries and rosemary sprig for garnish

1. Place the St. Germain, vodka, lemon juice, and simple syrup in a cocktail shaker filled with ice. Shake 15 seconds until cold. Strain into a Champagne flute.
2. Top off the glass with rosé Champagne. Thread 2 raspberries onto sprig of rosemary and place in the flute.

The Empress

Exotic and beautiful, this luscious cocktail is worthy of Empress Joséphine herself.

Makes 1 cocktail

2 ounces Empress 1908 Gin*
1 ounce vodka
2 ounces rosemary simple syrup (recipe on page 15)
1 ounce Meyer lemon juice, freshly squeezed

1. Place all the ingredients in a cocktail shaker filled with ice and shake vigorously until tiny shards of ice are suspended in the liquor.
2. Pour into a chilled cocktail glass.

*Empress 1908 Gin is made in Victoria, Canada, and available world-wide. It gets its distinctive color from butterfly pea blossoms.

Marie's Revenge

This sweet cocktail is the perfect sip and nibble for those who prefer to drink their dessert—and eat it too.

Makes 1 cocktail

1 ounce Chambord Raspberry Liqueur
2 ounces CÎROC French Vanilla Vodka
Garnish with a sparkling sugar rim and a store-bought *petit four*

1. Pour a little vodka in a shallow dish and sprinkle sparkling sugar in another. Dip the rim of a *coupe* cocktail glass in the vodka, then in the sugar.
2. Pour the Chambord and vodka into a cocktail shaker filled with ice; shake vigorously and pour into the glass.
3. Cut a slit (about ¼-inch deep) in the bottom of the *petit four* and perch it on the edge of the glass.

Waterloo

Napoleon was defeated at the Battle of Waterloo in 1815, but the grand little Emperor lives on through this signature Cognac cocktail. My sister-in-law Julie serves this potent cocktail at every DeRitis family gathering and it makes us all feel very tall!

Makes 1 cocktail

2 ounces Courvoisier Cognac
1 ounce Cointreau orange liqueur
¾ ounce Meyer lemon juice, freshly squeezed
Orange twist
2 Amarena cherries

1. Pour Courvoisier, Cointreau, and lemon juice into a cocktail shaker filled with ice. Cover, shake for at least 30 seconds, and pour into a *coupe* cocktail glass.
2. Garnish with an orange twist and 2 Amarena cherries.

Smoked Salmon with Avocado Crème Fraîche

This appetizer is ridiculously simple, yet so sophisticated. And when the occasion calls for something extra special, you can even add a dollop of caviar on top. I love the nuttiness of the avocado mixed with *crème fraîche*. It is also nice served as a unique condiment for roast chicken or pork.

Makes about 12 servings

1 ripe avocado, pitted, peeled, and roughly chopped
½ cup *crème fraîche* (recipe on page 76)
½ teaspoon sea salt
1 pound smoked salmon
Chives, minced

1. Place the avocado in the small bowl of a food processor; pulse until puréed. Add *crème fraîche* and sea salt. Purée until smooth.
2. Cut the smoked salmon into 1-inch cubes, top with the Avocado *Crème Fraîche* and sprinkle with minced chives. Avocado *Crème Fraîche* will keep in the refrigerator for 2–3 days (lay a piece of plastic wrap directly on top of the mixture to keep it from discoloring).

Pairing suggestion: Champagne or other sparkling wine

Camembert with Pears and Balsamic Pecans

Want an appetizer to serve at even the most sophisticated cocktail party? Here it is: opulent *Camembert* with luscious sautéed pear, and honey balsamic-glazed pecans.

Serves 6–8

¼ cup ADI Apicoltura Organic Orange Flower Honey ♥
1 tablespoon Ritrovo Selections Aged Balsamic Vinegar ♥,
    plus more for drizzling
1 teaspoon fresh thyme, minced, plus more for garnish
½ teaspoon sea salt
1 pinch Michele Ferrante *Controne* Hot Pepper ♥ (optional)
2 cups pecan halves
1 tablespoon salted butter
1 ripe pear, peeled and diced
1 8-ounce wheel of ripe *Camembert* cheese

♥*See favorite products section on pages 170–176.*

1. Line a baking sheet with parchment paper or a silicone baking mat.
2. Place honey, balsamic vinegar, thyme, sea salt, and pepper flakes in a heavy skillet set over medium heat. Stir to combine and add the pecans. Cook, stirring constantly, for about 4 minutes until the balsamic and honey are absorbed and pecans begin to brown (be careful they do not burn). Turn nuts out onto the lined baking sheet, separate them so they are not touching, and allow to cool. Roughly chop ½ cup of the candied nuts and set aside. Reserve 8–10 pecan halves for the garnish and store the remaining nuts in the refrigerator to use on salads or cheese platters.
3. Remove *Camembert* from refrigerator and cut in half horizontally, cover, and set aside to come up to room temperature (about 1 hour).
4. When ready to serve, place the butter in a small sauce pan and melt. Add the pears and sauté until just beginning to brown (4–5 minutes).
5. While the pears are still warm, arrange ½ of the *Camembert* on a serving plate (cut side up) and top with ½ of the pears and ¼ cup of the nuts. Drizzle with balsamic vinegar and top with the other round of cheese (cut side down). Top with remaining pears and ¼ cup of chopped nuts. Arrange pecan halves around top and drizzle with more balsamic vinegar. Garnish with thyme sprigs. Serve with *baguette* slices or crackers.

Pairing suggestion: Champagne or other sparkling wine

Notes

If you're in a hurry, use store-bought candied pecans for this delicious appetizer.

Comté Triangles

These wonderfully crisp crackers owe their great taste to (surprise!) butter and *Comté* cheese. Fresh thyme and a pinch of white pepper add zest. The long triangle shape is perfect for dipping and looks elegant fanned around a pot of Chicken Liver *Pâté* (pictured on opposite page).

Makes about 24 crackers

2 cups white whole-wheat flour (see notes)
1 tablespoon fresh thyme, leaves only
1 tablespoon sugar
1 teaspoon sea salt
¼ teaspoon white pepper
½ cup unsalted, cold butter, cut into ½-inch cubes
1 cup *Comté* cheese, finely grated
½ cup heavy cream
Extra virgin olive oil
Sea salt

Notes

White whole wheat is a type of wheat. It's 100% whole wheat— not a mixture of white and wheat flours, nor is it bleached. It contains a smaller amount of tannin than red wheat which makes traditional whole-wheat flour darker in color and heartier in taste. White wheat flour is lighter in color and flavor.

Several brands can be found in better grocery stores such as Bob's Red Mill, King Arthur Flour, and Trader Joe's.

1. Place the flour, thyme, sugar, sea salt, and pepper in the bowl of a food processor; pulse to combine.
2. Gradually add butter cubes, pulsing as they are added, until the mixture resembles coarse meal. Add the grated cheese, and pulse 2–3 times more.
3. With the processor running, pour in the heavy cream, and process just until it starts to form a dough.
4. On a lightly floured surface, briefly knead the dough and divide into 2 equal pieces, each shaped into a rectangle. Wrap in plastic wrap and refrigerate for 30–60 minutes.
5. Preheat oven to 375°F and line 2 baking sheets with parchment paper or silicone baking mats.
6. On a lightly floured surface, roll out the first piece of dough into a long, very thin rectangle. (About 7 x 5 inches and ⅛-inch thick). Using a pizza cutter or sharp knife, cut the dough into 2-inch-wide rectangles, then cut diagonally to create 2 triangle crackers. Repeat with second piece of dough.
7. Transfer the triangles to the prepared baking sheet. Brush each triangle with extra virgin olive oil and sprinkle with sea salt.
8. Bake for about 12–15 minutes, then turn the sheets back to front and continue baking for 8–10 minutes more until they are nicely browned.
9. Let the crackers cool completely before storing them in an airtight container. They will keep in the refrigerator for up to 2 weeks and can be frozen for up to 3 months.

Chicken Liver Pâté

Rich, buttery and delicious, this spread is a decadent addition to any cocktail party. I prefer using pear Cognac in this recipe because it adds a bit of sweetness; however, unflavored Cognac or brandy can be used as well. Serve the pâté with Comté Triangles (recipe on opposite page) and a glass of sparkling wine.

Makes about 2 cups

8 tablespoon unsalted butter, cut into 1 tablespoon slices, divided
⅓ cup shallots, minced
1 pound chicken livers, trimmed of fat and connective tissue
1 teaspoon sea salt
2 garlic cloves, minced
2 tablespoons capers
1 tablespoon fresh thyme
1 teaspoon anchovy paste
¼ cup pear-infused Cognac (see notes)
¼ cup cream
⅛ teaspoon white pepper

1. Heat 2 tablespoons of butter in a large sauté pan set over medium heat. Let the butter brown, about 3–5 minutes (do not let it burn).
2. Add the shallots and sauté for 2 minutes, then add the chicken livers. Space them out in the pan to allow room for cooking and sprinkle with salt. Turn the livers over when one side browns (about 4 minutes total cooking time).
3. Add garlic, capers, thyme, and anchovy paste; cook until livers are browned. Add the pear Cognac and increase the heat to high. Let it boil until reduced and caramelized (about 2 minutes). Turn off heat and allow to cool in the pan.
4. Once cooled, place the livers in the bowl of a food processor and pulse several times. Add butter, 1 tablespoon at a time, pulsing between each piece, then add the cream. Continue to pulse until the *pâté* is very creamy. The mixture may be loose, but it will thicken as it cools.
5. Divide mousse into small ramekins or a *pâté* dish, then refrigerate for at least 1 hour before serving.
6. Serve with *Comté* Triangles (recipe on opposite page) or *baguette* slices. The *pâté* can be covered in plastic wrap and stored in the refrigerator for 5 days and for up to 1 month if sealed with melted duck fat, clarified butter, or lard. Remove fat to serve.

Pairing suggestion: Champagne or other sparkling wine

Notes

It's easy to make your own pear-infused Cognac:

1 bottle Cognac
2 ripe Bosc pears, cored and cubed (do not peel)
1 cup sugar
1 cup water

Pour Cognac into a large jar and add half of the pear cubes. Add remaining pear, sugar, and water to a pot and boil for 15 minutes. Allow to cool, then pour it into the jar with Cognac.

Store in a cool dark place for 2 weeks. Strain Cognac through a fine mesh sieve into a sterilized bottle and compost the pear. Store in the freezer indefinitely. But be sure to sip a little while you're making the *pâté*.

Duck Confit and Grilled Peach Salad

This splurge salad features exotic duck *confit* and fresh fruit. The cherry balsamic dressing pairs beautifully with the saltiness of the duck and sweetness of the peaches and berries. For a special occasion, this dish will definitely impress your guests.

Serves 6

3 legs duck *confit* (see notes)

For the salad:
3 ripe peaches, cut in half and pitted
6 cups any mixture of European greens (radicchio, bibb lettuce, endive or fennel fronds)
2 cups fresh cherries (pitted and cut in half) and mixed berries, any combination
⅓ cup roasted almonds, roughly chopped

For the dressing:
3 tablespoons Ritrovo Selections Cherry Balsamic Vinegar ♥
1 teaspoon Casina Rossa Salt&Saluté ♥
¼ cup extra virgin olive oil
1 teaspoon fresh rosemary, minced
Freshly ground black pepper

♥*See favorite products section on pages 170–176.*

Notes

Duck *confit* is made by braising salted duck legs in fat. It can be found in specialty food markets and online. Smoked chicken or turkey can also be substituted in this recipe.

1. Remove the skin from the duck legs, take the meat off the bone, shred with a fork, and set aside.

Make the dressing:
2. Place the Cherry Balsamic Vinegar and Salt&Saluté in a small bowl and whisk together. Slowly drizzle in the extra virgin olive oil, while whisking. Once oil is emulsified, add the rosemary and pepper.

For the salad:
3. Brush the cut side of the peach halves with dressing and grill over medium heat, rotating a quarter turn halfway through, until heated through and browned (7–8 minutes). Set aside to cool.
4. Place the shredded duck in a small bowl and toss with about ¼ of the dressing.
5. Place the radicchio, greens, cherries, and berries in another bowl, toss with remaining dressing.
6. To assemble: Place a mound of the greens mix on each plate and top with one of the grilled peach halves (cut side up). Place a portion of the duck *confit* on top of the peach, scatter with some chopped roasted almonds and season with more of the Salt&Saluté if desired. Garnish with fresh fennel fronds or edible flowers. The salad is best if eaten the same day, but the duck *confit* mixture can be stored in the refrigerator for up to 5 days.

Pairing suggestion: Champagne, Granache, or Provençal rosé

Pink Pralines

These are a bit fussy to make, but one batch will go a long way.

Makes 2 cups

3 cups sugar
3 pinches sea salt
¾ cup water
Red food coloring
2 cups toasted almonds
2 teaspoons orange flower water

1. Line a large baking sheet with parchment paper or a silicone baking mat.
2. Place 1 cup of sugar, 1 pinch of sea salt, ¼ cup water, and a few drops of red food coloring in a large heavy skillet; mix well with a wooden spatula. Set over medium-high heat and bring to a boil. Once large bubbles start forming, add the toasted almonds. Lower the heat and continue to stir constantly and add the orange flower water. The red sugar syrup will begin to crystallize; keep stirring to coat the nuts thoroughly. Once the sugar stops adhering to the almonds, the nuts will look like they are covered with pink confectioners' sugar. Transfer the almonds onto the prepared baking sheet to cool. Collect the remaining pink sugar and place in a small bowl. This will be used in the second stage of cooking. Clean up the pan and spatula with hot water and dry.
3. Place the almonds in the cleaned skillet, reserving the parchment paper or silicone baking mat on the baking sheet.
4. In a small saucepan, place 1 cup of sugar, 1 pinch of sea salt, ¼ cup water, the reserved pink sugar, and a few drops of red food coloring. Allow to melt. Bring to a boil and cook until the temperature reaches 255°F (use a cooking thermometer). Transfer the pan with the almonds to the burner and pour the syrup over nuts, stirring at the same time. Once the almonds are coated well and look like they are covered with pink sugar, transfer them onto the parchment again. Separate nuts and pink sugar. Clean up the pan and spatula as before.
5. Repeat the last step one more time, using the remaining ingredients.
6. Place the sugared almonds on the baking sheet until cooled. Serve with cocktails or as a garnish for desserts. Almonds will keep in a well-sealed container in the refrigerator for 1 month or in the freezer for several months.

Notes

These beautiful pink sugared almonds are sweet, crunchy, and delicious—the perfect *petit* nosh for our Parisian-themed *soirée*.

A culinary tradition in the French city of Lyon, Pink Pralines can be used to decorate desserts or added to cakes, tarts, and even sweet specialty breads such as *brioche*.

Seasoned Crackers

Need a quick and easy nibble? Fill martini glasses or little bowls with these tasty crackers for snacking at your next party. Their crunchy flavor also enhances salads, soups, and chowders.

Makes 4 cups

½ cup butter, melted
1 garlic clove, minced
2 tablespoons *herbes de Provence* (see notes)
2 teaspoons sea salt
½ teaspoon white pepper
4 cups oyster crackers

1. Preheat oven to 275°F and line a large baking tray with parchment paper or a silicone baking mat.
2. Pour melted butter into a small bowl, then add garlic, *herbes de Provence*, sea salt, and white pepper. Whisk to combine.
3. Pour crackers into a 1-gallon freezer bag, drizzle in the butter mixture, and seal the bag. Shake so that crackers are coated with seasoning.
4. Pour the crackers onto the baking tray and spread evenly. Bake for 15–20 minutes, stirring after 10 minutes, until they have absorbed all the butter and are toasty brown. Allow to cool before storing in an airtight container.
5. Crackers can be stored in the refrigerator for up to 1 week or in the freezer for up to 4 months.

Notes

Any seasoning combination can be used in place of the *herbes de Provence* to make these savory crackers. Try garlic and Italian seasoning, or Greek seasoning.

Chocolate Pots de Crème

Because this is an extremely rich dessert, dainty portions are a fitting finale to our elegant Parisian-themed cocktail party.

Makes about 3 cups

2 cups whipping cream
½ cup whole milk
5 ounces bittersweet (but not unsweetened) or semisweet chocolate, chopped
6 large egg yolks
⅓ cup sugar
Hot water
Fresh raspberries and mint leaves for garnish

Notes

Have fun and get creative with serving dishes for these desserts. Oven-proof juice glasses, shot glasses, even *espresso*, or tea cups can be used.

1. Preheat oven to 325°F.
2. Place cream and milk in a heavy medium saucepan set over medium heat and cook until just beginning to simmer. Remove from heat.
3. Add chocolate pieces and whisk until melted and smooth. Set aside.
4. Place egg yolks and sugar in large bowl and whisk together. Gradually whisk in the hot chocolate mixture. Strain mixture through a fine mesh sieve into another bowl. Cool 10 minutes and skim any foam from the surface.
5. Divide custard mixture among six ¾-cup ramekins (see notes). Cover each dish with foil. Place cups in a large baking pan with 2-inch sides. Add enough hot water to pan to come halfway up sides of cups.
6. Bake until custards are set but centers still move slightly when gently shaken (about 55 minutes—if using smaller cups, the baking time will be less). Remove from water; remove foil. Chill in the refrigerator until cold firm, about 3 hours.
7. Serve topped with a fresh raspberry and a mint leaf. *Pots de Crème* can be made 2 days ahead of serving and will keep in the refrigerator (covered with foil) for up to 5 days.

Pairing suggestion: Pedro Ximenez Sherry or Rasteau Vin Doux Naturel

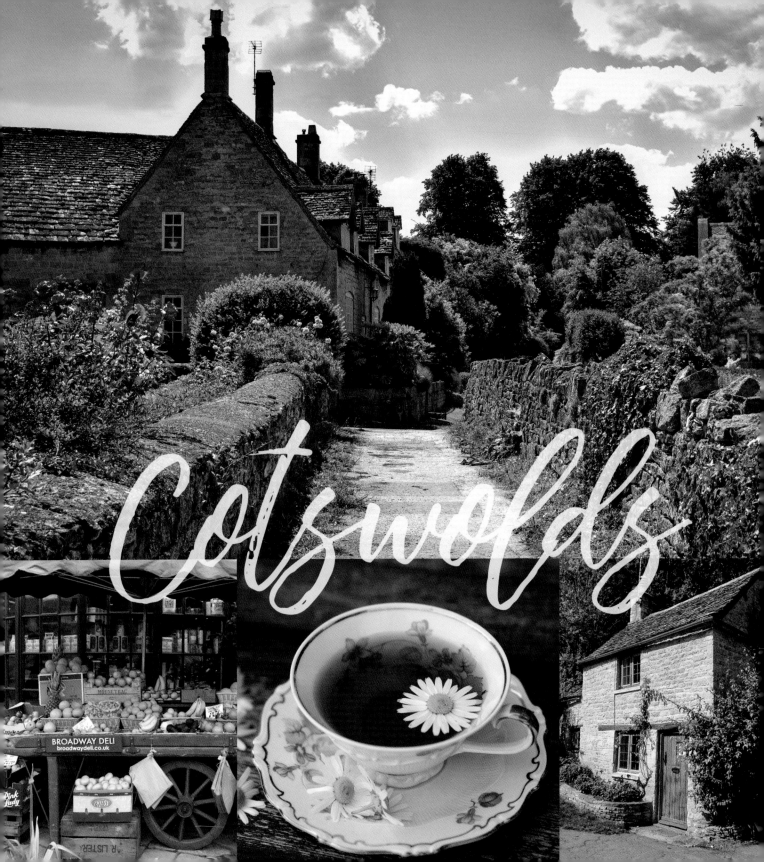

Cotswolds

A time-honored ritual, afternoon tea is served all over the British Isles. Cream teas include scones with clotted cream and jam, sandwiches and other savories, as well as tiny cakes. Located about two hours northwest of London, the Cotswolds are famous for their rolling hills and quintessentially English market towns built of honey-colored stone. Make this elaborate cream tea feast with your friends—and transport yourselves to a cozy thatched-roof cottage in a fairytale Cotswolds village.

Cream Tea
IN THE COTSWOLDS

The Scoop on Tea

While the custom of drinking tea was popularized in England during the 1660's, it was not until 1840 that "afternoon tea" was introduced by Anna, the seventh Duchess of Bedford. After becoming a tad *"peckish"* about four o'clock in the afternoon, she would order a little snack sent to her room. The Duchess began inviting friends to join her and "afternoon tea" became a fashionable social event. Today tea continues to be celebrated—and there are hundreds of teas from which to choose. A good selection for a cream tea party is one black tea and one green or herbal tea. Serve with lemon slices, sugar, and cream.

BLACK TEAS

Black tea is the most popular tea in Britain and a great choice for a tea party. The tea leaves are allowed to fully oxidize during processing, giving the tea leaves their dark color and rich aroma.

Assam is a strong tea known for its full-bodied malty flavor, deep aroma, rich color, and brisk taste.
Ceylon is a medium-bodied tea with a citrus flavor.
Darjeeling is a light, delicate tea perfect for cream teas.
Earl Grey is a blend of *Keenum* tea and bergamot oil.
English Breakfast Blend is a perfectly balanced blend mix of *Assam, Ceylon,* and *Kenyan* teas.
Keenum is one of the most famous types of black tea, with a mellow, fruity aroma and flavor. It is often described as wine-like.
Lapsang Souchong is perhaps the most famous of China teas. It has a smoky aroma and flavor.
Yunnan has a rich, earthy taste similar to *Assam* and makes an excellent breakfast tea.

GREEN TEA

Green tea is barely oxidized at all, so the leaves keep some of their originally vibrant green color and fresh-picked flavor.

Jasmine is scented with the aroma of jasmine blossoms: beautifully fragrant, and subtly sweet.
Dragon Well or *Longjin* is a light, delicate, sweet, and nutty tea referred to by both names.

OOLONG

Oolong is a partially oxidized tea with lighter, fruitier flavors than black teas.

Da Hong Paois has a strong aroma, deep dark red color, and a distinctively fruity, earthly, and sweet flavor.
Ti Kwan Yin or *Tie Guan Yin* is a lightly oxidized tea with a sweet, floral flavor.
Formosa features the flavors of flowers, peaches, and a bit of spice. It's a nice choice for afternoon tea.
Alishan is a creamy and refreshing tea with a strong yet sweet aftertaste.

HERBAL TEAS

As the name suggests, herbal teas are not made from tea, but from blends of herbs, flowers, and spices.

Chamomile is a daisy-like plant that has a component called *chrysin* which acts as a sleep aid.
Peppermint is one of the most commonly found herbal teas, and is often used to support digestive health.
Hibiscus is made from flowers of the hibiscus plant. It has a pink-red color and raspberry-citrus flavor which is lovely for afternoon tea.
Rooibos is made from the leaves of the *rooibos* or red bush plant which grows in South Africa. It offers smoky, sweet, vanilla, floral, and honey flavors.
Lemon Balm is herbal and light, with a lemony flavor.
Rose Hip is made from the fruit of the rose plant. High in vitamin C, it offers tart citrus and floral flavors.

Gin with Homemade Tonic

This classic British cocktail is traditionally served with a slice of lemon or lime—or both. Who knew that making homemade tonic syrup is so easy? Mix it with an herbaceous gin such as Hendrick's Midsummer Solstice for a summertime refresher anytime.

Makes 1 cocktail

1 tablespoon Homemade Tonic Syrup (recipe on opposite page)
2 ounces gin
2 ounces sparkling water
Lemon or lime wedge

1. Fill an old-fashioned glass with ice. Add 1 tablespoon (or more to taste) of the tonic syrup to each glass, add 2 ounces gin, and top with sparkling water. Stir to combine.
2. Serve with a generous squeeze of lemon or lime, or both.

Pimm's Cup

Originating as a health drink in 1840's London, Pimm's Cup is a cocktail classic. This gin-based *digestif* is bitter, herbaceous, and makes a refreshing summer drink mixed with ginger ale or lemonade.

Makes 1 cocktail

2 ounces Pimm's No. 1
6 ounces ginger ale*
Lemon, cucumber, strawberries, and mint sprigs for garnish

1. Pour the Pimm's No. 1 into a cocktail glass filled with ice and top with ginger ale.
2. Garnish with any combination of lemon, cucumber, strawberries and mint sprigs.

*Lemon-lime soda or lemonade may also be used as the mixer.

Homemade Tonic Syrup

This tonic makes a fabulous cocktail mixed with gin or vodka. It's also wonderful added to sparkling water for a non-alcoholic *aperitif*. The bitterness of the *cinchona* bark balances nicely with the citrus, lavender, and cardamom. *Cinchona* is a tree native to South America and its bark has been used medicinally for centuries to prevent malaria, increase appetite, treat bloating, and other stomach problems—so go ahead and have two tonic cocktails! Here's to your health!

Makes 1½ liters of tonic

For the tonic:
3 cups water
¼ cup chopped *cinchona* bark (see notes)
¼ cup citric acid
Zest of 3 limes, 3 lemons, and 3 navel oranges
3 stalks lemongrass, tops and bottoms trimmed, washed thoroughly and outer leaves removed, sliced into ½-inch rounds (see notes)
4 whole allspice berries
4 whole juniper berries
4 whole green cardamom pods
1 tablespoon lavender buds
1 tablespoon dried rose petals
¼ teaspoon sea salt

For the simple syrup:
3 cups sugar
1½ cups water

For the tonic:
1. Place all ingredients, except simple syrup, in a sterilized, 1-quart lidded glass jar. (I like to use Euro-style canning jars as they are functional, beautiful, and you never have to search for the lids.) Shake to combine. Refrigerate for 72 hours, shaking occasionally, at least once per day.

For the simple syrup:
2. Dissolve 3 cups sugar in 1½ cups water over medium heat until all sugar is completely dissolved. Allow to cool. Transfer to a container and refrigerate.
3. After 72 hours of steeping, use a mesh sieve and strain tonic mixture into a large glass pitcher. Strain tonic a second time, using a coffee filter or very fine cheesecloth.
4. Stir simple syrup into tonic and mix until thoroughly combined.
5. Pour tonic into sterilized glass bottles and store in the refrigerator for up to 4 weeks. Tonic can also be frozen for up to 6 months. I also like to portion it out into ice cube trays and freeze so it can be easily added to cocktails.

Notes

Cinchona bark can be found from several online retailers. Be sure to order the chopped *cinchona* version. Lemongrass can be found at most Asian markets.

Caramel Slices

In Scotland, they call these Millionaire Bars. But whatever you call these rich cookies, they are possibly the best dessert ever created! A crispy shortbread crust with creamy caramel, topped with semisweet chocolate ganache, and sea salt—nothing's better with a cup of tea.

Makes 24 squares

For the shortbread crust:
1 cup unsalted butter, softened
⅓ cup sugar
½ cup light brown sugar, firmly packed
1 large egg yolk
1 teaspoon vanilla extract
2¼ cups unbleached all-purpose flour
½ teaspoon sea salt

For the caramel:
2 14-ounce cans sweetened
    condensed milk
14 tablespoons unsalted butter, cut
    into ¼-inch slices
1 cup light brown sugar, firmly packed
⅓ cup light or dark corn syrup
1 teaspoon vanilla extract
¼ teaspoon sea salt

For the chocolate ganache:
2 cups semisweet chocolate, cut
    into small chunks
½ cup heavy cream
½ teaspoon vanilla extract
Sea salt for sprinkling

For the shortbread crust:
1. Preheat oven to 350°F. Line a 9 x 13-inch cake pan with parchment paper or a silicone baking mat.
2. Using a stand mixer fitted with a paddle attachment, beat butter until well creamed. Add sugars and beat until light and fluffy (about 30 seconds). Add egg yolk and vanilla extract and stir well, pausing to scrape down the sides until ingredients are well combined.
3. Mix the flour and salt together, then add gradually, ½ cup at a time, to the butter mixture until slightly crumbly.
4. Firmly press dough evenly into prepared baking pan. To make it easier, lay a piece of wax paper or plastic wrap over the dough and use a metal measuring cup to pat down the mixture evenly. Bake for 20–25 minutes until edges are lightly golden. Set aside to cool while preparing caramel topping.

For the caramel:
5. Place a medium-sized saucepan over medium heat and add the condensed milk, butter, brown sugar, and corn syrup.
6. Stir frequently until butter is melted and ingredients are well combined. Continue stirring for several minutes until mixture begins to boil. Continue cooking for 10–15 minutes until it thickens and turns a rich caramel color. The caramel will begin pulling away from the sides of the pan.
7. Remove from the heat. Stir in the vanilla extract and salt, then pour evenly over the prepared shortbread. Cool in the refrigerator for at least 1 hour before topping with chocolate ganache.

For the chocolate ganache:
8. Place chocolate chunks in a glass bowl. Heat the heavy cream in a small saucepan over medium heat until about to boil. Pour the hot cream over the chocolate and stir until all the chocolate is melted. Stir in vanilla extract and allow chocolate to cool just slightly, then evenly spread over the prepared caramel layer and sprinkle with sea salt.
9. Place pan in the refrigerator and allow chocolate to harden before removing from the pan, cutting, and serving. Bars can be stored for up to 1 week in the refrigerator.

Shortcut "Clotted Cream"

Traditional clotted cream takes at least 12 hours to prepare in a temperature-controlled environment. This shortcut version is equally tasty and just takes a few minutes to make. Serve it with scones and jam or as a topping for tarts or pies.

Makes 2½ cups

4 ounces cream cheese, softened
1 cup sour cream
3 tablespoons confectioners' sugar
1 cup heavy whipping cream

1. Place cream cheese in the bowl of a stand mixer fitted with a paddle attachment and beat until fluffy. Add sour cream and confectioners' sugar; mix until well combined.
2. Slowly add the cream with the mixer on medium until stiff peaks form. Refrigerate and serve cold. This "Clotted Cream" can be stored in the refrigerator for up to 2 weeks.

Lamb Pies

Meat pies with hot-water crust are hearty and delicious. In the Middle Ages, the crusts were thick, hard, and not meant to be eaten—they were really just a vessel for the filling. But I promise, this recipe makes very tasty crusts. And don't be frightened by the lard. It adds a flavor and texture that simply cannot be duplicated with butter or vegetable shortening.

Makes 6 pies

For the gravy:
2 tablespoons unsalted butter
2 tablespoons unbleached
    all-purpose flour
1 cup beef broth

For the filling:
1 pound leg of lamb, cut into 2-inch
    chunks (or lean ground lamb)
1 yellow onion, peeled and minced
3 garlic cloves, peeled
1 tablespoon Worcestershire sauce
4 teaspoons fresh winter savory
    (see notes on page 110) or
      1 tablespoon rosemary, minced
½ teaspoon nutmeg, freshly ground
½ teaspoon salt
½ teaspoon black or red pepper
1 cup gravy

For the pastry:
4 cups "00" ♥ or unbleached
    all-purpose flour, add more
    if necessary
1 teaspoon sea salt
¾ cup lard (see notes on page 110)
¾ cup water

For the egg wash:
1 large egg, beaten with
    1 tablespoon water

♥ *See favorite products section on pages 170–176.*

For the gravy:
1. In a small saucepan over medium heat, melt the butter, add the flour, and whisk together until smooth. Whisk in the broth, a little a time. Set aside to cool.

For the filling:
2. Place lamb pieces in the bowl of a food processor and pulse until the meat is chopped into small pieces slightly larger than ground beef. Remove to a large mixing bowl and set aside. Add onion and garlic to the meat mixture. Stir in the Worcestershire sauce, winter savory or rosemary, nutmeg, salt, pepper, and gravy. When the meat is well mixed, refrigerate until ready to use.

For the pastry:
3. Preheat the oven to 400°F and line a large baking sheet with parchment paper or a silicone baking mat. Place 6 English muffin rings on the baking sheet.
4. In a large bowl, whisk together the flour and salt. Make a well in the center. In a small saucepan over medium heat, bring the lard and water to a boil. Pour into the well and stir until combined and cool enough to touch.
5. Turn the dough out onto a lightly floured surface, knead 4–5 minutes until the dough is smooth, adding more flour a little at a time as needed. The dough should be easy to handle—not sticky or crumbly. Cut off a ⅓ of the dough and place in a pan with the lid on to keep it warm. Pat the remaining dough flat and gently roll it ¼-inch thick. Using a small plate or saucer as a template, cut out 6 circles (6 inches each) of dough, gathering the scraps and re-rolling, as necessary.
6. To assemble: Pat the circles of dough into the prepared rings, gently pushing down and into the sides. There should be about ½ inch of dough sticking up around the edges; let hang over the outside of the rings as you use this to seal the edges of the pies.
7. Divide the cooled filling between each lined muffin ring, filling all the way to the top.

Recipe continues on next page.

Notes

Winter savory is a perennial thyme-like herb used for centuries to flavor meat and game.

Lard can be found in the baking section of most grocery stores. I prefer Morrell Snowcap or Armour brands.

8. Roll the reserved dough ¼-inch thick and cut out 6 circles (3½ inches each). Cut small vent holes in the circles to allow steam to escape while the pies are baking. (Tip: Use a large round piping tip to cut a vent hole in the center.)
9. Place the lids over the meat filling and fold the outside edges back over the tops, pinching them to stand up around the edge. If you have extra dough, cut out shapes to decorate the tops of the pies. Patch and pinch where necessary to make sure they are well sealed.
10. Gently lift rings from the pies and allow them to stand on their own.
11. Brush the tops and sides of the pies with the egg wash and bake for 50–60 minutes, until golden brown. Remove the pies from the oven and serve warm.
12. Serve with afternoon tea or as a light winter supper. There probably won't be any leftovers—but if there are, wrap in plastic and store in the refrigerator for up to 1 week or freeze for up to 3 months.

Suggested paring: Claret or Côtes du Rhône red

Lemon Curd

Makes 1½ cups

½ cup lemon juice, freshly squeezed
½ cup sugar
3 large eggs
6 tablespoons salted butter, cut
    into ½-inch cubes
2 teaspoons lemon zest

1. In a heavy saucepan set over medium-low heat, combine the lemon juice, sugar, and eggs. Whisk until combined. Stir in butter and cook, stirring often, until curd is thick enough to hold marks of whisk, about 6 minutes.
2. Place a fine-mesh sieve over a small bowl, add the curd, and stir until mixture is strained.
3. Stir in the lemon zest and place a piece of plastic wrap directly on top of the curd.
4. Chill in the refrigerator for at least 1 hour. The curd will continue to thicken as it cools.
5. Lemon curd can be stored in the refrigerator for up to 1 week and in the freezer for 2–3 months.

Lemon Lavender Tartlets

Such a classic Cotswolds combination: lemon and lavender. These little bites are crisp and zesty—and a lovely addition to afternoon tea or a celebration brunch.

Makes 32 tartlets

2¾ cups unbleached all-purpose flour
½ cup white whole-wheat flour
    (see notes on page 92)
½ teaspoon sea salt
½ teaspoon baking soda
½ teaspoon cream of tartar
1 tablespoon culinary lavender
    buds, minced
½ cup butter, room temperature
½ cup sugar
1 cup confectioners' sugar
½ cup avocado oil
1 egg
1 teaspoon lemon extract
1 teaspoon vanilla extract
Confectioners' sugar for decorating
Lemon curd

1. Preheat oven to 350°F.
2. In a large bowl, combine the flours, salt, baking soda, cream of tartar, and lavender; set aside.
3. In the bowl of a stand mixer fitted with a paddle attachment, cream the butter and sugars together until light and fluffy. Beat in the oil, egg, and extracts, then add flour mixture, a little at a time, until well combined.
4. Grease a mini muffin tin with butter, drop 1 tablespoon of dough (a small cookie scoop works perfectly for this) into each cup. Bake for 10 minutes.
5. Remove from oven and, using the end of a wooden spoon handle, make an indentation in the center of each ball of dough. Fill with a teaspoon of lemon curd. Return to the oven and bake for 8–10 minutes more, until cookies are firm and lightly browned. Remove muffin tin to a wire rack to cool. Make sure tartlets are thoroughly cooled before removing from pan.
6. Sprinkle the edges of the cookies with confectioners' sugar and top with more lemon curd. Lemon tartlets can be stored in the refrigerator for up to 1 week.

Orange-Glazed Cream Scones

Traditionally served with fruit preserves and clotted cream, these petite cream scones are flaky and delicious with a nutty flavor thanks to the addition of walnuts. I like to serve them with my shortcut version of clotted cream (recipe on page 108) and raspberry jam.

Makes 16 scones

For the scones:
2 cups unbleached all-purpose flour
½ cup walnuts, toasted and
    roughly chopped
2 teaspoons baking powder
1 tablespoon sugar
½ teaspoon salt
6 tablespoons unsalted butter,
    cut into ½-inch chunks
2 large eggs, well beaten
½ cup plus 1 tablespoon heavy cream
2 teaspoons orange zest
Optional: pearl sugar, raw sugar, or
    poppy seeds for the top

For the glaze:
¼ cup confectioners' sugar
1 teaspoon orange juice,
    freshly squeezed
1 teaspoon orange zest

Notes

Scone variations:
Add ¾ cup of currants, dried cranberries, mini chocolate chips, or chopped candied ginger. For zesty scones, add 1 tablespoon of orange or lemon zest.

For the scones:
1. Preheat oven to 425°F.
2. Line a baking sheet with parchment paper or a silicone baking mat.
3. In the bowl of a food processor, pulse together the flour, walnuts, baking powder, sugar, and salt until walnuts are finely chopped and incorporated into the flour mixture.
4. Drop in the butter, 1 chunk at a time, pulsing until just incorporated.
5. Add eggs, 1 at a time, and ½ cup of the cream; pulse until dough comes together. Do not overwork.
6. Turn dough out onto a lightly floured surface and separate it into 2 equal pieces. Form each half into a ball and flatten into a circle about ¾-inch thick and 5 inches in diameter. Cut each circle into 8 pie-shaped wedges. Place wedges about 1 inch apart on the prepared baking sheet. Brush tops with remaining cream (and sprinkle with sugar or poppy seeds if desired).
7. Bake on the center rack of the oven for 12–15 minutes, or until lightly browned. Cool for 5 minutes on the pan and then transfer to a cooling rack. Place the baking sheet below the baking rack before glazing to catch the drips.

Glaze the scones:
8. In a small bowl, whisk together the confectioners' sugar, juice, and zest. Brush over warm scones and allow to sit for a few minutes. Serve with Shortcut "Clotted Cream" (recipe on page 108) and jam. Scones can be stored in an airtight container in the refrigerator for up to 1 week.

Pear Balsamic Chutney

This chutney's sweet and savory flavors perfectly complement Stilton *Gougéres* (recipe on opposite page). I also like to serve this unique chutney with roasted pork or poultry—or as a tasty sandwich spread.

Makes 1½ pints

2 ripe *d'Anjou* pears, peeled, cored,
    and roughly chopped
2 tablespoons lemon juice, freshly squeezed
2 tablespoons extra virgin olive oil
½ cup shallots, finely chopped
½ cup light brown sugar
1 garlic clove, minced
1 teaspoon fresh ginger, minced
    (or ½ teaspoon dried ginger)
½ teaspoon cinnamon
½ teaspoon sea salt
⅛ teaspoon Michele Ferrante *Controne* Hot Pepper ♥
¼ cup golden raisins, roughly chopped
¼ cup Ritrovo Selections Organic Apple
    Balsamic Vinegar ♥
¼ cup walnuts, toasted and roughly chopped
2 teaspoons fresh thyme, minced

♥ *See favorite products section on pages 170–176.*

1. In a small bowl, toss the pears with the lemon juice. Set aside.
2. Set a heavy saucepan coated with the olive oil over medium heat. Add the shallots and sauté until shallots turn transparent but are not browned. Add the pears, brown sugar, garlic, ginger, cinnamon, salt, and red pepper flakes, then simmer for an additional 5 minutes.
3. Stir in golden raisins and balsamic vinegar; simmer for about 10 minutes, until the liquid has evaporated and chutney thickens.
4. Add the walnuts and thyme; mix until just heated through. Remove from heat and allow to cool in the pan.
5. The chutney can be stored in a sealed jar in the refrigerator for up to 1 month or frozen for up to 3 months.

Stilton Gougères

Similar to popovers, these little puffs of deliciousness melt in your mouth. The tangy saltiness of the Stilton cheese partners beautifully with the Pear Balsamic Chutney (recipe on opposite page) drizzled with apple balsamic vinegar. This recipe makes an elegant appetizer with cocktails, or as a highlight of an afternoon tea party.

Makes 12 gougères

2 large eggs
1 cup whole milk
2 tablespoons unsalted butter, melted, plus more for greasing tins
1 cup unbleached all-purpose flour
½ teaspoon sea salt
⅛ teaspoon Michele Ferrante *Controne* Hot Pepper ♥
1¼ ounces Stilton cheese, crumbled
1 tablespoon fresh thyme, minced
Ritrovo Selections Apple Balsamic Vinegar ♥

♥*See favorite products section on pages 170–176.*

1. Place the eggs, milk, melted butter, flour, salt, and red pepper flakes in a large bowl. Whisk until all lumps have disappeared. Stir in the cheese and thyme. Transfer the batter to an airtight container and refrigerate for at least 2 hours, or up to 1 day before baking. The batter must be well chilled before baking.
2. Preheat the oven to 425°F. Generously butter a mini muffin or popover pan. Fill each cup to the top with the chilled batter (using a measuring cup to pour the batter helps).
3. Bake until golden brown and puffed, about 15–18 minutes. Serve the *gougères* warm drizzled with Apple Balsamic Vinegar, Pear Balsamic Chutney and a wedge of Stilton cheese.
4. *Gougères* are best served the same day they're baked, but will keep for a few days in the refrigerator. Reheat to serve.

Pairing suggestion: Dry Riesling or sparkling wine

Tuscany

The curated hills of Tuscany offer one of the most spectacular landscapes in the world. I'm not Italian, but every time I visit this legendary region, I feel like I am coming home. The cuisine here is seasonal—fresh, simple and *delizioso*!

Evening
IN TUSCANY

Tuscan Lemon Drop

I love how rosemary simple syrup adds such an herbal freshness to the classic lemon drop cocktail. Just one sip and I'm instantly transported to the Tuscan countryside.

Makes 1 cocktail

3 ounces lemon-flavored vodka such as Absolut
2 ounces Meyer lemon juice, freshly squeezed
1 ounce Rosemary Simple Syrup (recipe on page 15)
Lemon slice
Sparkling sugar for the rim

1. Fill a large cocktail shaker with ice, pour in all drink ingredients and shake vigorously.
2. Rub a lemon slice around the rim of a cocktail glass, dip in sugar and fill the glass.
3. Sprinkle a few lavender buds or rosemary leaves on tops of the drink if desired. Garnish with a lemon slice.

Bresaola e Rucola

Cured Beef with Arugula

Bresaola is lean beef tenderloin cured with wine, salt and spices. Available at gourmet grocery and specialty stores, this thinly sliced meat elevates a simple salad to something truly remarkable. The combination of *bresaola* and fresh arugula is also a popular pizza topping in Italy.

Serves 4

20 thin slices of *bresaola*
1 large bunch of arugula
***Parmigiano-Reggiano* cheese, shaved**
Extra virgin olive oil
Ritrovo Selections Aged Balsamic Vinegar ♥ or lemon wedges
Sea salt
Freshly ground black pepper

♥See favorite products section on pages 170–176.

1. Remove *bresaola* from refrigerator and bring to room temperature. Arrange 5 slices in a circle on each of 4 salad plates.
2. Place a small mound of arugula on top of the *bresaola*.
3. Distribute *Parmigiano-Reggiano* cheese shavings over the salads.
4. Drizzle olive oil and balsamic vinegar or lemon juice on each salad. Sprinkle with a little sea salt and freshly ground black pepper.

Pairing suggestion: Chianti Classico

Schiacciata di Pomodori Secchi

Tuscan Focaccia Bread with Sun-Dried Tomatoes

This bread is easy to make and loaded with lots of flavorful olive oil. I like to top it with sun-dried tomatoes, roasted vegetables, or fresh herbs. It's also wonderful as part of a meat and cheese board, or for *panini*.

Makes one 9 x 13-inch Focaccia

2 cups warm water (110–115°F)
4 teaspoons active dry yeast
1 tablespoon sugar
5 cups bread flour
1 tablespoon sea salt, plus
    more for finishing
Extra virgin olive oil
½ cup sun-dried cherry tomatoes
1 tablespoon fresh rosemary
1 tablespoon *Parmigiano-Reggiano*
    cheese, shredded

1. Place the warm water in a small bowl and sprinkle with the yeast and sugar. Let dissolve for about 10 minutes, until yeast begins to activate.
2. Place flour and salt in a large bowl, whisk to combine, and make a hole in the middle.
3. Once the yeast mixture is ready, pour it slowly into the well in the flour mixture, stirring with a fork to mix.
4. When all the water and yeast are incorporated into the flour, turn it out onto a floured board and knead for about 10 minutes. If necessary, add more flour to the dough. It should be slightly sticky.
5. Grease a large bowl with a little olive oil, drop the dough in and cover with plastic wrap. Place the bowl in a warm spot and let the dough rise for about 1½ hours or until doubled in size.
6. Punch down dough, turning it inside out. Knead a few times, cover, and let rise for an additional 20–30 minutes.
7. Preheat oven to 350°F.
8. Brush a 9 x 13-inch baking dish with olive oil (just enough so the dough won't stick). Settle the dough into the pan, working it by hand and pushing it in with fingertips to evenly distribute. Top with the sun-dried cherry tomatoes, gently pushing them into the surface. Sprinkle with fresh rosemary and sea salt.
9. Cover entire surface with olive oil so it won't dry out when baking. Let rise for about 20 minutes more.
10. Bake bread for about 15 minutes and then sprinkle with the shredded *Parmigiano-Reggiano*. Continue baking for another 10–15 minutes until golden brown on top. If the sun-dried tomatoes begin to burn, cover loosely with foil for the last few minutes of baking.
11. Allow bread to cool in the pan for a few minutes, then remove from pan and place on a cooling rack. This will help keep the bottom crispy. Serve with more extra virgin olive oil and balsamic vinegar if desired.
12. This bread is best fresh, but can be wrapped in foil and stored at room temperature for 3–4 days.

Tagliatelle con Tartufo
Tagliatelle with Truffles

Black truffles and rich egg pasta—truly one of the most delicious combinations imaginable! My tour group enjoyed this decadent dish with our friends Roberto and Maria Grazia at Mannucci Droandi Winery in Tuscany (*MannucciDroandi.it/en*). *Tagliare* means "to cut" in Italian, thus *tagliatelle* is a "cut" of pasta. It can be made using the *fettuccine* roller of pasta machines, or by loosely rolling the thin dough into a log and cutting it by hand with a very sharp knife.

Serves 8

2 cups "00" ♥ or unbleached
    all-purpose flour
2 cups semolina flour
1 tablespoon sea salt, plus more
    for cooking pasta
6 large eggs
2 tablespoons olive oil
½ cup heavy cream
Freshly ground black pepper
Parmigiano-Reggiano cheese, grated
1 whole black truffle, shaved
    (see notes)

♥*See favorite products section on pages 170–176.*

Notes

Fresh truffles are not always available so preserved black truffles or truffle sauce can also be used.

1. Sift flours together with salt onto a work surface. Form a mountain out of flour mixture and make a deep well in the center. Break the eggs into the well and add the olive oil. Whisk eggs very gently with a fork, gradually incorporating flour from the sides of the well. When mixture becomes too thick to mix with a fork, begin kneading with your hands. A bench scraper helps with this. (Pasta dough can also be made using a food processor fitted with the metal blade. Be sure to add eggs 1 at a time and blend after each addition, before adding oil.)

2. Once the dough becomes smooth and somewhat stiff, lightly flour a work surface and continue kneading for 8–10 minutes more, until the dough becomes elastic. (Dust the work surface and your hands with flour if necessary.) Divide the dough into 4 pieces and flatten into small rectangles sized to fit through the pasta machine. Wrap in plastic, and set aside for 30 minutes at room temperature to rest.

3. Using either a manual or electric pasta machine, adjust the rollers to the widest setting (this setting is usually "0"). Working with 1 rectangle of dough at a time, feed the dough through the rollers. Remove and lightly dust with semolina flour. Fold the strip into thirds, flatten with your fingertips, and pass it through the machine at least twice more. The dough should be very smooth and the edges should be even. Dust with semolina if dough becomes sticky. Once the pasta is smooth, do not add additional flour.

4. Adjust the pasta roller to the next setting ("1") and pass the dough through once again. Continue reducing the thickness settings and rolling the dough until it is as thin as needed (about $\frac{1}{16}$ inch which is usually the "5" setting on most pasta machines). As the strips become increasingly longer, take care not to pull or stretch them. The easiest way is to gently hold the strip of dough between your left thumb and forefinger while cranking with your right hand—or better yet, recruit a second pair of hands!

Recipe continues on next page.

5. Cut the pasta strips into 18-inch lengths. Cover the strips with a clean cloth and let them rest for 10–15 minutes. Run the pasta sheets through the *spaghetti* or *fettuccine* roller to cut. Alternately, pasta sheets can be sprinkled with semolina, rolled up loosely, and cut with a sharp knife to desired width.

6. If not cooking the pasta immediately, spread it on clean, dry towels lightly dusted with flour, tossing to separate the strands. You can also hang it over a pasta drying rack or the back of a kitchen chair. Repeat with remaining dough. At this point, pasta can be flash-frozen on baking trays and transferred to freezer bags, then frozen for up to 3 months.

7. To cook the pasta, set a large pot half full of water seasoned with 1–2 tablespoons of sea salt over medium heat. Bring to a rolling boil.

8. Add the pasta and then immediately begin to stir gently so that the noodles do not stick together. Continue to cook until the pasta is *al dente* (cooked through, but firm: 3–4 minutes if using fresh pasta, 5–8 minutes for dried, and 8–10 minutes if frozen).

8. Drain the pasta, reserving some of the water in another container. Return pasta to the burner and stir in the butter pieces and cream. Season with sea salt and freshly ground pepper to taste. Add pasta water, a few tablespoons at a time, until the sauce is emulsified with the *tagliatelle*. (If using preserved truffles or truffle sauce, add them at this stage.)

9. Transfer to a serving bowl and top with *Parmigiano-Reggiano* cheese and freshly shaved black truffles.

Pairing suggestion: Tuscan Sangiovese such as Mannucci Droandi Chianti, or Brunello di Montalcino

Tuscan Roasted Potatoes

Crispy potatoes are a popular side dish in Tuscany—and everywhere else. I especially like the color and texture of Yellow Finn potatoes for this recipe, but russet or unpeeled red potatoes are delicious as well.

Serves 8

3 pounds Yellow Finn potatoes, peeled and cut into 1½–2-inch chunks

¼ cup extra virgin olive oil

2 tablespoons lemon juice, freshly squeezed

3–4 garlic cloves, minced

1 tablespoon fresh sage, finely chopped

1 tablespoon fresh rosemary, finely chopped

1 tablespoon Italian flat-leaf parsley, finely chopped

1–2 teaspoons sea salt

1 teaspoon freshly ground black pepper

***Parmigiano-Reggiano* cheese**

Zest of 1 lemon

1. Preheat oven to 425°F.
2. Place potato pieces in large baking dish and arrange in a single layer.
3. Place olive oil, lemon juice, garlic, sage, rosemary, parsley, sea salt, and pepper in a small bowl; whisk to combine. Pour over the potatoes and toss to coat.
4. Roast for 20 minutes and remove from oven. Using a spatula, turn potatoes and return to oven.
5. Cook for an additional 15–20 minutes or until potatoes are crispy.
6. Remove from oven, adjust seasoning, and top with *Parmigiano-Reggiano* cheese and lemon zest. Potatoes will keep in the refrigerator for 5–7 days.

Tagliata con Balsamico
Rib-Eye Steak with Balsamic Vinegar

This savory steak is found in every *trattoria* in Tuscany. Boneless rib-eye is the classic choice for this dish, but it can also be made with Porterhouse, New York, or tenderloin cuts. Italians enjoy their salt so don't skimp on the seasonings—you won't regret it.

Serves 8

For the steaks:
**4 aged boneless rib-eye steaks,
    about 2 inches thick**
2 tablespoons extra virgin olive oil
**2 tablespoons fresh rosemary,
    finely chopped**
**2 tablespoons fresh sage,
    finely chopped**
2 garlic cloves, minced
Sea salt
Freshly ground black pepper

For the salad:
3 cups fresh arugula
½ cup extra virgin olive oil
**3 tablespoons Ritrovo Selections
    Aged Balsamic Vinegar ♥,
    plus more for serving**
Sea salt & freshly ground black pepper
***Parmigiano-Reggiano* cheese, shaved**

♥*See favorite products section
on pages 170–176.*

For the steaks:
1. Remove steaks from the refrigerator, pat dry and brush all sides with olive oil.
2. Place herbs and garlic in a small bowl; mix to combine and then rub steaks with the herb mixture. Season liberally with sea salt and freshly ground pepper to taste. Allow to come up to room temperature before cooking (1–2 hours).
3. Preheat oven to 450°F.
4. Place a heavy skillet over medium-high heat. Once the skillet is hot, sear the steaks 3–4 minutes on each side until well browned.
5. Tip steaks up on end, leaning them against the side of the pan (this helps to keep the juices in the meat). Place steaks in the oven and roast until internal temperature reaches 120–130°F for rare or 130–135°F for medium rare (12–20 minutes depending on thickness of the steaks).
6. Remove from oven, cover with foil, and allow to rest for 5 minutes.

For the salad:
7. Arrange arugula on a serving platter, drizzle with olive oil and vinegar, then season with sea salt and freshly ground pepper to taste.
8. Slice steak into thin strips (about ¼-inch thick) and arrange over the arugula salad. Top with shaved *Parmigiano-Reggiano* cheese and drizzle with more balsamic vinegar. Steak will keep in the refrigerator for up to 5 days. Leftovers are wonderful in *paninis* or served in salads.

Pairing suggestion: Bold Italian red wine such as Brunello di Montalcino, Chianti Classico, Sagrantino, or Super Tuscan

Crostata di Mele

Apple Crostata

Nothing says autumn like apple pie—and this rustic *crostata* is my Italian version. The delicate crust has the surprising addition of *Parmigiano-Reggiano* cheese in honor of my father who always declared, "Apple pie without the cheese is like a kiss without the squeeze!" I like to sauté the apples prior to baking so they are soft and delicate. The hazelnut crumble topping adds sweetness and crunch.

Serves 6

For the pastry:
1 cup "00" ♥ or all-purpose flour
2 tablespoons sugar
¼ cup *Parmigiano-Reggiano*
  cheese, grated
¼ teaspoon sea salt
½ cup unsalted butter, cold, cut
  into ½-inch chunks
1 teaspoon cold vodka
2 tablespoons ice water

For the filling:
1 tablespoon unsalted butter
3 large Honey Crisp or McIntosh
  apples, peeled and thinly sliced
1 tablespoon sugar
1 tablespoon orange juice,
  freshly squeezed
1 tablespoon orange zest
¼ teaspoon freshly grated nutmeg

For the topping:
¼ cup flour
¼ cup sugar
¼ teaspoon sea salt
¼ teaspoon ground cinnamon
⅛ teaspoon ground allspice
4 tablespoons cold unsalted
  butter, diced
¼ cup hazelnuts (or walnuts),
  roughly chopped

♥*See favorite products section on pages 170–176.*

For the pastry:
1. Place the flour, sugar, *Parmigiano-Reggiano* cheese, and salt in the large bowl of a food processor fitted with a steel blade. Pulse a few times to combine.
2. Add the butter, 1 chunk at a time, and pulse several times, until the butter is the size of peas.
3. With the motor running, gradually pour the vodka and ice water through the feed tube. Keep pulsing to combine. Stop the machine just before the dough becomes a solid mass.
4. Turn the dough onto a well-floured board and form into a disc. Wrap in plastic and refrigerate for at least 1 hour.
5. Preheat oven to 450°F and make the filling.

For the filling:
6. Place butter and apples in a large heavy skillet set over medium heat and sauté 5–10 minutes until apples begin to soften but are still firm.
7. Gently stir in sugar, orange juice, orange zest, and nutmeg. Set aside.

For the topping:
8. Combine flour, sugar, salt, cinnamon, and allspice in a bowl of a food processor fitted with a steel blade.
9. Add the butter and pulse until mixture is crumbly.
10. Pour into a bowl and rub with your fingers until it starts holding together. Mix in hazelnuts and set aside.

Form the crostata:
11. After the pastry has been chilled for 1 hour, place on a floured surface and roll into an 11-inch circle.
12. Arrange apple slices in the middle of the pastry, leaving a 1½-inch border.
13. Sprinkle topping evenly over apple slices.
14. Gently fold the crust over to enclose the apples, pleating it to form a circle.
15. Bake for 30–40 minutes until the crust is golden and the apples are tender. Serve warm or at room temperature with vanilla bean ice cream. *Crostata* will keep in the refrigerator for 5–7 days.

Pairing suggestion: Vin Santo

Provence

For centuries, artists and gourmets have flocked to Provence for its stunning scenery and magical light, as well as its *cuisine du soleil* featuring an abundance of fresh produce, herbs, and olive oil. I can imagine no better place for a picnic than on a grassy hillside with a view of lavender fields and vineyards. Indulge with a crusty *baguette*, platter of French cheese and chilled bottle of rosé—even if you're only dreaming in your backyard.

Picnic
IN PROVENCE

Rosé, the Perfect Picnic Wine

A pink wine made from red grapes, rosé's color can range from pale orange to a darker purple—depending on the grapes and wine-making techniques. Rosé has enjoyed a renaissance in recent years as wine lovers have discovered French-style rosé. This versatile wine pairs with many dishes but is especially delightful with picnic fare. Here's a selection of my top picks for affordable, approachable, and food-friendly rosés. Ask your local wine merchant to order them for you.

FRANCE

Bandol Rosé
Domaine Les Luquettes, $25
From the Bandol area of Provence, made with *Mourvéedre* and *Cinsault*. Rich copper in color with aromas of fruit and white flowers. Full-bodied with flavors of mandarin, grapefruit, and black pepper. It is delicious with *pâté,* cured meats, and aged cheeses. *Imported by IolaWines.com.*

IGP Mont Caume Rosé
Domaine Les Luquettes, $20
From the Bandol area of Provence, made with *Cinsault, Cabernet Sauvignon,* and *Sauvignon Blanc*. Pale peach in color with elegant perfume of white flowers, *agrume,* and passion fruit. Delicate yet concentrated on the palate with subtle notes of apricot and generous notes of exotic fruit. Structured and well-balanced with pleasing length. It pairs well with *charcuterie, tapenade,* and tomato-based dishes. *Imported by IolaWines.com.*

La Bastide des Oliviers Provence Rosé
Patrick Mourlan Coteaux Varois en Provence, $15–$17
From Provence, made with *Cinsault, Grenache, Carignan,* and Syrah. Pale pink in color with aromas of golden raspberries, Rainier cherries, and wild strawberries. Brisk, crisp, and elegant, this authentic *Provençal* rosé satisfies on all levels. *Imported by PetitMondeWine.com.*

L'Hermas
Matthieu Torquebiau, $18–$22
From the Languedoc region of southern France, made with 100% *Grenache*. Pretty pale pink color, this dry rosé tastes of fresh fruit and pairs well with Mediterranean cuisine. *Imported by PetitMondeWine.com.*

Domaine Montrose
Bernard et Olivier Coste, $14–$16
From the Languedoc region of southern France, made with *Grenache, Cabernet Sauvignon,* and *Syrah.* Pale pink in color with notes of fresh berries, it tastes of red berries and peaches with spicy overtones. Lovely on its own and delicious with seafood and creamy cheeses. *Imported by PetitMondeWine.com.*

Sancerre Rosé, Cave de la Bouquette
Thierry Véron, $19–$22
From the Loire Valley in central France, made with 100% *Pinot Noir*. Deep pink in color, with aromas of fresh berries. With a light and delicious fruity favor, this wine is a perfect match for cured meats, *pâté,* and cheeses. *Imported by PetitMondeWine.com.*

Wispering Angel Rosé
Chateau d'Esclans, $20–$22
From the Côte de Provence region of southern France, made with *Grenache, Cinsault,* and *Rolle* (*Vermentino*). Pale coral pink in color with tangy pink grapefruit aromas, it tastes of citrus, melon, and peaches. An elegant choice for a *charcuterie* board and any *al fresco* meal. *Imported by esclans.com*

WASHINGTON

Le Rosé
Hedges Family Estate, $17–$22
From the Red Mountain area of eastern Washington, made in the French style with Syrah, *Mourvédre,* and *Counoise*. This is my favorite Washington rosé. Le Rosé is a beautiful picnic wine with a brilliant coral color. It tastes light and fruity with hints of citrus, melon, and rose petals, and has a creamy finish. *Produced by HedgesFamilyEstate.com.*

Fromages
Secs
Riquet   1,50 €/l
Beffroi   2,00 €/l
Rigole) 2,50 €/l
Brique)

Fromages

No proper *Provençal* picnic would be complete without a sumptuous selection of cheese. There's no set rule as to how many to include, but three different styles make a good start. France boasts 360 cheese AOCs (*Appellation d'Origine Contrôlée* or "Controlled Designation of Origin," which was developed to protect the authenticity of each *fromage*). More than 1,600 varieties are available, so you have plenty of choices. Below are several of my favorites to include in a picnic. *For more information about French cheese, visit cheese.com.*

SOFT CHEESES

Brie de Meaux is made from unpasteurized cow's milk from the village of Meaux This *Brie* has a milky rich taste with sweet and buttery flavors reminiscent of mushrooms or truffles and almonds.

Camembert de Normandie is a raw cow's milk cheese from Normandy and perhaps my favorite French cheese. It has a smooth, runny interior and a white bloomy rind that make it a perfect mate for *pâté* .

Fromager D'Affinois is a cow's milk cheese from the Rhone-Alpes region reminiscent of a triple-crème *Brie*, but the flavor is more mild with a buttery quality and sweetness that pairs well with fresh fruit.

Époisses is a French word meaning "completely worth the effort." Made from cow's milk in the Côte-d'Or region of Burgundy, this cheese is a tad stinky but velvety smooth, delicious and oh, so worth it.

SEMI-HARD CHEESES

Morbier is a cow's milk cheese named after the village of Morbier in the Franche-Comté region. Pungent and nutty with a signature layer of vegetable ash running down the middle, this cheese is a delightful addition to any picnic.

Tomme des Pyrénées is made from cow and sheep milk in the Midi-Pyrénées. This mild, buttery cheese is an all-time favorite. It can be difficult to find in the U.S., but it is well worth the search.

Tomme de Savoie is a cow's milk cheese from the Rhone-Alpes region. This tomme is creamy and light because it is made from the skim milk left over after the cream is used to make butter or richer cheeses.

HARD CHEESES

Beaufort is a firm, raw cow's milk cheese that is in the Gruyère family. An Alpine cheese, it is produced in the Savoie region of the French Alps.

Comté is made from unpasteurized cow's milk in the Franche-Comté province of eastern France. *Comté* has the highest production of all French AOC cheeses.

BLEU CHEESES

Bleu d'Auvergne is a French blue cheese named after its place of origin in the Auvergne region of south-central France. Made from either raw or pasteurized cow's milk, this cheese is sometimes considered the cow's milk version of *Roquefort*, although its consistency is much creamier and buttery.

Roquefort is from the caves of Combalou in southern France, and arguably the world's greatest blue cheese. Made from sheep's milk, its name and methods have been protected since 1411. *Roquefort's* heavenly flavor is sharp, sweet, and peppery.

GOAT'S MILK CHEESES

Bûcheron is a cheese from the Loire Valley that offers a complete trifecta of flavors. A firm lemony middle is wrapped in creamy goodness, and the edible rind provides a sharp contrast.

Crottin is a staple of central France that perfectly pairs tanginess and creaminess. Only mildly "goaty," it has a bloomy scent like fresh mushrooms with a nice balance of salt and acid.

Aubergine "Caviar"

Eggplant Spread

Known as "poor man's caviar," this spread is much more delicious than it is photogenic. And it contains no actual caviar! Quick, healthy, and easy to prepare, it's wonderful slathered on a crusty *baguette* or crackers.

Makes about 1½ cups

2 medium eggplants
1 head of garlic
2 tablespoons fresh parsley, chopped
1 tablespoon fresh thyme, minced
2 tablespoons lemon juice, freshly squeezed
¼ cup extra virgin olive oil
½ teaspoon sea salt
⅛ teaspoon Michele Ferrante *Controne* Hot Pepper ♥ (optional)
Fresh parsley for garnish

♥See favorite products section on pages 170–176.

1. Preheat the oven to 400°F and line a baking sheet with foil.
2. Poke each eggplant a few times with a sharp knife. Cut one-quarter off the top of the head of garlic, drizzle with olive oil, and cover with foil. Place eggplants and garlic on the baking sheet; bake 20–30 minutes. Remove the garlic head and set aside to cool. Continue baking the eggplants until tender (about 10–15 minutes more).
3. When cool enough to handle, cut the eggplants in half lengthwise, scoop out the flesh and place in the bowl of a food processor. Squeeze the garlic cloves into the mixture and pulse until almost blended. Add the parsley, thyme, lemon juice, extra virgin olive oil, sea salt, and hot pepper flakes. Pulse until well blended. Add sea salt and hot pepper to taste.
4. Serve on *baguette* (recipe on page 141) slices or crackers and garnish with parsley. This *Aubergine Caviar* will keep in the refrigerator for up to 5 days.

Black and Green Tapenade

A pungent *Provençal* spread, *tapenade* is made from black olives, capers, and anchovies. In this recipe I combine both *Taggiasca* and *Castelvetrano* olives to help mellow the sharp flavors slightly.

Makes about 1 cup

½ cup *Taggiasca* olives
½ cup *Castelvetrano* olives, pitted
1–2 garlic cloves, minced
¼ cup fresh Italian parsley, chopped
1 teaspoon capers
1 teaspoon anchovy paste (see notes)
2–3 tablespoons extra virgin olive oil
Fresh Italian parsley for garnish

1. Place olives, garlic, parsley, capers, and anchovy paste in the small bowl of a food processor; pulse several times until well chopped.
2. Drizzle in extra virgin olive oil gradually while pulsing. Serve on *baguette* (recipe on page 141) slices or crackers and garnish with parsley. *Tapenade* will keep in the refrigerator for up to 5 days.

Notes

Make your own anchovy paste by mashing anchovy fillets that have been packed in olive oil.

Cherry Shallot Confiture

Similar to a chutney, this savory *confiture* pairs perfectly with *pâté* and French cheeses—especially *Brie* and *bleu*. I love it served with chicken or pork as well.

Makes ½ pint

2 tablespoons extra virgin olive oil
⅓ cup shallots, minced
2 cups Bing cherries, pitted
2 tablespoons lemon juice, freshly squeezed
⅓ cup sugar
2 teaspoons orange zest
2 tablespoons Ritrovo Selections Amarena Cherry Balsamic ♥
1 teaspoon Casina Rossa Fiori&Salt ♥, or more to taste
⅛ teaspoon Michele Ferrante *Controne* Hot Pepper ♥

♥See favorite products section on pages 170–176.

1. Pour extra virgin olive oil into a heavy skillet and sauté the shallots over medium heat until translucent and just beginning to brown.
2. While the shallots are cooking, place the cherries in the bowl of a food processor and pulse until they are chopped, but not puréed.
3. When the shallots are cooked, add the cherries, lemon juice, and sugar. Simmer, stirring occasionally, until all the liquid has been absorbed (about 15 minutes).
4. Add the orange zest and the Amarena Cherry Balsamic; continue to simmer a few minutes more until thickened.
5. Add Fiori&Salt ½ teaspoon at a time, to taste, and the hot pepper flakes if desired.
6. Serve with grilled meats, *charcuterie*, or cheeses. *Confiture* will keep in the refrigerator for up to 1 month and in the freezer for up to 3 months.

Classic Baguettes

Crunchy, chewy and delicious, *baguettes* are ideal for a picnic—or anytime! Classic French *baguettes* are made from only four ingredients: water, yeast, flour, and salt. This recipe uses a sourdough starter or *poolish*. Don't let this intimidate you. It is an extra step, but it's not difficult and helps to create the most flavorful bread.

Makes 3 baguettes

For the starter (poolish, see notes on page 142):
1½ cups lukewarm water
⅛ teaspoon active dry yeast
 or instant yeast
1 cup unbleached all-purpose flour

For the baguettes:
1½ cup warm water, 110–115°F
1 tablespoon active dry yeast
1 cups starter
3½ cups bread flour, plus
 more for kneading
2 teaspoons sea salt
Extra virgin olive oil
1½ cup boiling water

For the starter:
1. Place all ingredients in a small bowl and mix thoroughly. Cover loosely with a tea towel and let rest at room temperature overnight. Starter should have expanded slightly and be bubbly.

For the baguettes:
2. Place warm water in a large mixing bowl and sprinkle yeast on top; set aside for 10–15 minutes and allow yeast to activate (it will start to bubble).
3. Mix in the sourdough starter, then add the bread flour, and sprinkle salt on top. Mix in the bowl until a dough forms. Turn out onto a floured surface and knead until smooth and elastic, adding flour as needed (10–15 minutes). Dough should be slightly sticky. A stand mixer with a dough hook can be used, but I prefer kneading bread by hand. It is very therapeutic and good exercise too.
4. Oil a large bowl or a 4-quart plastic storage container with a little extra virgin olive oil, place the ball of dough in the bowl, and turn over so top is coated with oil. Cover with a tea towel (or seal lid on storage container) and let rise until doubled in bulk (1½–2 hours, or longer depending on ambient temperature).
5. Punch the dough down, turning it inside out, re-form the ball and place back in the bowl, covered, for an additional 1½–2 hours. Again, it should double in bulk.
6. Divide dough into 3 equal pieces (using a scale helps with this) and form each into a rectangle (about 4 inches wide and 6 inches long). Tightly roll each rectangle of dough from the short side into a 4-inch log and press edges of dough with side of hand to seal. With the seam side down, gently roll the dough into a 16-inch log, tapering each end to a point.
7. Place the logs seam-side down on a lightly-floured surface (about 3 inches apart to allow for rising) and sprinkle with flour. Cover with a tea towel and allow to rise and puff up slightly (about 45 minutes).

Recipe continues on next page.

Notes

Poolish is a pre-ferment or starter consisting of a simple mixture of flour, water, and a leavening agent (typically yeast or a sourdough culture). After mixing, it is allowed to ferment for a period of time, and then added to bread dough as a substitute for— or in addition to—more yeast.

Pre-ferments are critical for the best tasting breads. Called a *biga* in Italian or sponge in Britain, they all do the same job—the difference just being their ratios of flour to water.

8. Preheat oven to 450°F. Line a baking sheet with parchment paper or a silicone baking mat and sprinkle with flour. (A baking stone can also be used. Sprinkle it with flour; no need for parchment paper.) Gently transfer the *baguettes* to the baking sheet, cover with a tea towel, and allow to rest for an additional 10–15 minutes.

9. Place a cast iron skillet or baking pan on the lowest rack of oven and allow to heat. Pour water into a small saucepan set over medium-high heat until it boils.

10. Using a baker's lame (a curved razor blade) or a very sharp knife held at about a 45° angle, make 3 diagonal slashes in each *baguette*.

11. Place the *baguettes* on the middle rack of oven. Carefully pour the boiling water into the skillet or baking pan on the lower rack, and quickly shut the oven door. The steam created by the boiling water will help the *baguettes* to rise and give them a crispy crust.

12. Bake 25–30 minutes, or until the loaves are a deep golden brown and sound hollow inside when tapped. Remove them from the oven and set the pan on a cooling rack. Cool 10–15 minutes before serving.

13. *Baguettes* are best eaten the same day as they are baked, but can be stored overnight in a paper bag, or wrapped in foil and frozen for up to 3 months. Thaw and reheat just before serving.

Gazpacho with Saffron Vodka Drizzle

Chilled soups are perfect for picnics, and *gazpacho* is a favorite in southern France. The saffron-infused vodka drizzle adds vibrant color and a surprising layer of deliciousness.

Serves 8

5 large ripe tomatoes (or one
  28-ounce can of peeled *San
  Marzano* Tomatoes ♥)
2 medium Persian cucumbers, peeled
  and roughly chopped
1 celery stalk, chopped
1 yellow pepper, de-seeded and
  roughly chopped
1 red pepper, de-seeded and
  roughly chopped
1 sweet onion, roughly chopped
2 garlic cloves, peeled and
  roughly chopped
½ cup extra virgin olive oil
Juice of 1 lemon or large lime
Sea salt to taste
1 teaspoon Michele Ferrante
  Controne Hot Pepper ♥ (optional)
Cilantro leaves, stems removed
  and roughly chopped
Saffron-infused Vodka (recipe
  on page 62)

♥ *See favorite products section
on pages 170–176.*

1. If using fresh tomatoes, remove the tops and place in a large pot of boiling water for 40 seconds or so. Remove the tomatoes from the water and let them cool for a few minutes. When they are cool enough to handle, gently remove the skins. (If using canned tomatoes, skip this step.)
2. Place tomatoes, cucumbers, celery, peppers, onion, and garlic in the bowl of a food processor or blender and pulse until puréed. With the food processor running, gradually pour in the olive oil, then add the lemon or lime juice. Pulse for a few seconds then add the salt, and red pepper flakes, and blend.
3. Test the *gazpacho* for seasoning. If it's too thick, add a little water and blend again until you reach the desired consistency.
4. Transfer the *gazpacho* to a glass bowl or jug and cover. Refrigerate for a couple of hours, or overnight for a more developed flavor.
5. When ready to serve, give the *gazpacho* a quick stir then transfer to small bowls or canning jars. Drizzle with Saffron-Infused Vodka and sprinkle with fresh cilantro. Soup will keep in the refrigerator for up to 5 days.

Pâté de Campagne

If you can make meatloaf, you can make this delicious French country *pâté*. I add *prosciutto* for texture and flavor, then stud it with *cornichons* so each slice is polka-dotted with bursts of crunchy tartness. Serve with *baguette* slices, soft cheeses, and Dijon mustard.

Makes about 24 slices

¾ cup Cognac
3 tablespoons unsalted butter
1 cup onion, minced
2½ pounds ground pork
12 ounces bacon (8–10 slices),
    finely chopped, plus 14 slices
    (for lining pan)
4 ounces *prosciutto*, finely chopped
3 garlic cloves, minced
2½ teaspoons sea salt
2½ teaspoons dried thyme
1½ teaspoons allspice
1 teaspoon freshly ground
    black pepper
2 large eggs, lightly beaten
⅓ cup whipping cream
1 jar *cornichons*
Boiling water
Dijon mustard or creamed
    horseradish for serving

1. Set rack at lowest position in oven and preheat to 325°F.
2. Place Cognac in a small saucepan set over medium heat and boil until reduced to ½ cup (2–3 minutes). Cool to room temperature.
3. Melt butter in a heavy skillet set over medium heat. Add onion and sauté until soft and translucent but not browned (about 8 minutes).
4. Place ground pork, chopped bacon, and *prosciutto* into a large bowl. Using fork or fingertips, mix until well blended.
5. Add sautéed onion, garlic, sea salt, thyme, allspice, and pepper to pork mixture and stir until combined. Add eggs, cream, and reduced Cognac. Stir or mix with hands until well blended.
6. Line a 12 x 4 x 3-inch loaf pan with bacon slices—arrange slices across width of pan, overlapping slightly. Lightly and evenly press ¼ of meat mixture onto bottom of pan on top of the bacon slices. Arrange a single layer of *cornichons* (about 15) lengthwise in rows about ½ inch apart on top of the pork. Top with ⅓ of remaining meat mixture; press down and arrange another row of *cornichons* on top. Continue with the last layer and top with remaining meat mixture. (When the finished *pâté* is sliced, there will be 3 neat rows of *cornichon* rounds.)
7. Fold bacon slices over, enveloping *pâté*. Cover pan tightly with foil. Place loaf pan in a 13 x 9 x 2-inch baking dish and transfer to oven. Pour boiling water into baking dish so it comes halfway up sides of loaf pan. Bake *pâté* until a thermometer inserted into center registers 155°F (about 2 hours and 15 minutes).
8. Remove loaf pan from baking pan and discard the water. Put loaf pan back in the baking pan and place heavy skillet (or 2 to 3 heavy cans) on top of the *pâté* to weigh it down. Chill in the refrigerator overnight.
9. When ready to serve, pour hot water into the baking pan and let sit for a few minutes. Invert *pâté* onto a platter. Wipe off any excess fat and discard.
10. Cut *pâté* crosswise into ½-inch slices and serve with Dijon mustard or creamed horseradish. *Pâté* can be made 4 days ahead and it is better if it sits for a few days in the refrigerator before serving. It can be stored in the refrigerator for 7–10 days.

Truffled Mushroom Galettes

These individual *galettes* are perfect picnic fare; they're also lovely paired with a salad for a light lunch or served as a starter for a celebration meal. The *Gruyère* cheese in the pastry offers a nutty contrast to the earthy mushrooms and creamy *ricotta*, with just a hint of truffle.

Makes 4 small galettes

For the pastry:
2 cups "00" ♥ or unbleached
    all-purpose flour
½ teaspoon sea salt
¼ cup *Gruyère* cheese, grated
¼ cup unsalted butter, cold, cut
    into ½-inch pieces
¼ cup lard, cold, cut into ½-inch pieces
1 tablespoon cold vodka (see notes)
4–6 tablespoons ice water

For the filling:
2 tablespoons extra virgin olive oil
4 cups *crimini* mushrooms (about
    12 medium mushrooms), sliced
1½ teaspoons Casina Rossa
    Truffle&Salt ♥, divided
⅛ teaspoon white pepper
¼ cup dry white wine
1 cup whole-milk *ricotta* cheese
¼ cup *Gruyère* cheese, grated
1 large egg, beaten
1 teaspoon water
Casina Rossa Extra Virigin Olive Oil
    with Black Truffle ♥

♥*See favorite products section
on pages 170–176.*

Notes

Adding vodka to pastry dough helps limit the formation of gluten, so crusts are flakier.

For the pastry:

1. Place the flour and salt in the bowl of a food processor; pulse to mix, add the cheese, and pulse to combine. Add the butter and lard gradually, pulsing until little ball shapes are formed. Add vodka and water (1 tablespoon at a time) then pulse just until the dough comes together. Remove dough to a floured surface, knead lightly, and shape into a ball. Wrap with plastic and refrigerate for at least 30 minutes.

For the filling:

2. Place a large skillet over medium heat and add the extra virgin olive oil. Heat until oil starts to smoke and then add the sliced mushrooms. Add 1 teaspoon of the Truffle&Salt and the white pepper. Cook until mushrooms have absorbed their juices (about 10 minutes). Add the white wine and continue to cook until mushrooms have absorbed all liquid (about 5 minutes). Set aside.

3. Place *ricotta*, *Gruyère*, and ½ teaspoon of Truffle&Salt in a small bowl. Mix thoroughly and set aside.

4. Preheat oven to 350°F and line a large baking sheet with parchment paper or a silicone baking mat.

5. Remove pastry from refrigerator and divide into 4 equal pieces. Form 1 portion into a ball, place on a floured surface, and roll out into an 8-inch circle, about ⅛-inch thick. Lay on the prepared baking sheet. Repeat for remaining pastry.

6. Spread each crust with ¼ of the *ricotta* mixture, leaving a 1 inch border. Arrange ¼ of the mushrooms on top. Fold crust over filling, pleating it to form a circle.

7. In a small bowl, whisk the egg and water together, then brush the mixture on the pastry. Drizzle filling with Casina Rossa Extra Virgin Olive Oil with Black Truffle.

8. Bake for about 55–60 minutes, rotate pan and cover *galettes* loosely with foil after about 30 minutes of baking to prevent mushrooms from burning. Serve warm or at room temperature. *Galettes* will keep in the refrigerator for 4–5 days. Reheat to serve.

Macarons with Apricot Basil Buttercream

These classic gluten-free cookies are found all over France in hundreds of different flavors. Yes, they are a little tricky to make—but just follow the directions closely and you'll have melt-in-your-mouth cookies. And, as I tell my family, "Even the ugly ones taste delicious!"

For the macarons:
1¾ cups confectioners' sugar
1 cup almond flour
3 large egg whites
¼ teaspoon cream of tartar
¼ cup sugar
1 teaspoon vanilla extract
1 teaspoon vanilla powder (see notes)
A few drops food coloring (see notes)

For the buttercream:
1 cup salted butter, softened
4–5 cups confectioner's sugar
¾ cup Apricot Basil Preserves
(recipe on page 49)

Notes

Vanilla powder adds an additional layer of vanilla flavor without adding extra moisture, but it can be easily omitted.

For the pretty peach color of the *macarons* pictured here, I used approximately 3 drops of orange and 1 drop of red food coloring, but any color can be used.

Any flavor of jam can be used in the buttercream.

For the macarons:
1. Line two baking sheets with parchment paper or silicone baking mats.
2. Combine confectioners' sugar and almond flour in the bowl of a food processor. Process for 30–40 seconds, until mixture has a very fine and light texture. Sift mixture twice into a large bowl and set aside.
3. Place egg whites in the bowl of a stand mixer fitted with whisk attachment; beat on medium-high speed until soft peaks form. With mixer running, add the cream of tartar and sugar (1 tablespoon at a time). Continue whipping until stiff peaks form, then add vanilla extract and vanilla powder (if using) and mix until incorporated.
4. Using a large spatula, gently fold about ⅓ of the almond flour mixture into egg whites, being careful not to overmix. Add another ⅓ and fold in; repeat with the last portion. The final mixture should be smooth and glossy and form a "V" shape as batter falls off of the spatula. Add a few drops of food coloring and mix until just combined.
5. Transfer batter to a piping bag fitted with a large round tip. Pipe 2-inch circles, about an inch apart, on both baking sheets. Tap baking sheets on the counter several times to release air bubbles. If air bubbles are visible, use a toothpick to poke the bubbles and smooth the cookies.
6. Let the *macaron* shells rest in a dry place for 20–30 minutes—until you can touch the shells without the batter sticking to your fingers. This is an important step in order for the classic "foot" of the *macaron* to form when baking.
7. Preheat oven to 325°F. Place 1 baking sheet of cookies on bottom rack of the oven and bake 14–16 minutes until edges of cookies can be gently lifted from parchment. Cool completely on baking sheet (about 20 minutes). Repeat for remaining cookies. Gently remove *macarons* from parchment paper and set aside.

For the buttercream:
8. Place the butter in the bowl of a stand mixer fitted with paddle attachment and beat until fluffy. Add confectioners' sugar, a little at a time, and mix until icing is stiff. Add the preserves; mix and add more confectioners' sugar until the buttercream is the desired consistency.
9. Place the buttercream in a pastry bag fitted with a large star tip. Pipe filling onto half of the cookies (about 1 tablespoon per cookie); top with remaining cookies to form a sandwich. Give the top cookie a little twist to secure it. *Macarons* are best eaten within 3 days, but can be stored in a tightly sealed container in the refrigerator for up to 7 days.

Sicily

Goethe said, "To have seen Italy without having seen Sicily is not to have seen Italy at all, for Sicily is the clue to everything," and I wholeheartedly agree. The island's agrarian tradition and multicultural history have influenced its delectable cuisine—featuring some of the most flavorful fruits, vegetables, and seafood in the world. Gather your friends and enjoy a taste of a bountiful Sicilian summer with this menu.

Summer
IN SICILY

Prickly Pear Granita

Served all over Sicily, *granitas* are icy treats made from fresh fruit, lemon juice, and sugar. Prickly pear cacti grow wild on the island, and are eaten raw or used to make jams and syrups. *Granitas* are generally non-alcoholic, but why not add some spirits and make a slushy cocktail? It's *bellissima!*

Makes 1 cocktail

3 ounces vodka
2 ounces *limoncello*
2 ounces lemon juice, freshly-squeezed
1 ounce prickly pear syrup (see notes)
1 cup, or more of ice
Prickly pear or lemon slice for garnish

1. Place all ingredients in a blender. Blend until slushy, adding more ice as needed.
2. Garnish with a prickly pear or lemon slice and a sprig of mint.

Notes

Sicilian Prickly pear syrup is difficult to find in the United States, but it is popular in the Southwest and can be found in specialty food markets and online. I prefer Cheri's Desert Harvest brand which is made in Arizona.

Fried Castelvetrano Olives

Castelvetrano olives are Italy's most ubiquitous snack olive. Bright green and mild, they are *Nocerella del Belice* olives that are grown near the village of *Castelvetrano*, on the western coast of Sicily. Fried snacks are popular in Sicily and these stuffed olives are a delightful cocktail nosh.

Makes 24 olives

24 *Castelvetrano* olives, pitted
2 anchovy fillets, cut into
    12 pieces each
1 ounce fontina cheese, cut
    into 24 slivers
½ cup flour
½ cup Italian beer, room temperature
½ teaspoon Michele Ferrante
    Controne Hot Pepper♥
Olive oil for frying
Toothpicks

♥*See favorite products section on pages 170–176.*

1. Stuff each olive with a little piece of anchovy and a sliver of *fontina* cheese. Skewer each with a toothpick and set aside.
2. Place flour in a small bowl and slowly whisk in the beer until the batter is smooth. Stir in the red pepper flakes.
3. Pour olive oil in a small skillet to about 1-inch depth and heat to 350°F.
4. Holding onto the end of the toothpick, dip each olive into the batter and coat evenly. Place in the heated oil and fry until golden brown. Serve warm. These snacks do not keep, but there won't be any left to worry about.

Pairing suggestion: Prosecco or other sparkling wine

Panelle with Sun-Dried Tomato Aioli

Chickpea Fries with Sun-Dried Tomato Aioli

A popular street food in Sicily, *panelle* are thin rectangles of chickpea batter fried in olive oil and served as an appetizer or vegetarian panini filling. In Liguria these delicious fries are called *panisse*. The shape of these chickpea "fries" creates the optimal crispy surface—perfect for dipping in the Sun-Dried Tomato Aioli.

Serves 6–8

For the chickpea fries:
1½ cups chickpea flour (see notes on page 19)
3 cups water
1 teaspoon coarse sea salt
2 tablespoons fresh parsley, finely chopped
1 tablespoon fresh rosemary, finely chopped
⅛ teaspoon of *Controne* Red Pepper Flakes ♥, or freshly ground black pepper
Olive oil for frying
Parmigiano-Reggiano cheese, and more parsley for garnish
Sea salt

For the sun-dried tomato aoli:
3 tablespoons sun-dried tomatoes, packed in oil
1 garlic clove, roughly chopped
1 cup good-quality mayonnaise
Casina Rossa Herbs&Salt ♥
⅛ teaspoon *Controne* Red Pepper Flakes ♥ or freshly ground black pepper

♥*See favorite products section on pages 170–176.*

For the chickpea fries:
1. Line a small baking sheet (approximately 12 x 15-inch) with parchment paper. Fold paper at the corners to line the sides of the pan also.
2. Pour the chickpea flour, water, and salt in a medium-sized saucepan and whisk until smooth. Set over medium heat and whisk constantly as the mixture slowly heats. Cook and keep whisking, scraping the bottom and sides of the pan frequently, until the mixture is smooth, thick, and starts to pull away from the sides of the pan (about 5 minutes). Remove from heat and quickly stir in parsley, rosemary, and red pepper flakes.
3. Pour the mixture onto lined baking sheet and spread quickly with an off-set spatula (before it cools and sets) so it fills the pan in an even layer, about ⅜-inch thick. Let cool in the refrigerator until completely firm (about 1 hour).
4. Once cooled, remove the chickpea mixture from the pan, by lifting the parchment paper and place on a cutting surface. With a sharp knife, cut into "fries" about ½ x 3-inches.
5. Pour olive oil into a large heavy skillet (enough to cover the bottom to a depth of ¼ inch) and set over medium heat. When the oil is hot, fry the panelle about 3 minutes, until the underside is crisp and golden, then flip and brown the other side (about 2–3 minutes more). Place the *panelle* on paper towels to drain excess oil. If needed, cook in batches. Sprinkle lightly with sea salt and *Parmigiano-Reggiano* cheese and serve hot with sun-dried tomato *aioli*. *Panelle* can be refrigerated for up to 1 week and reheated in extra virgin olive oil before serving.

For the sun-dried tomato aioli:
6. Place the sun-dried tomatoes and garlic in the small bowl of a food processor and pulse until finely minced, then add the mayonnaise; pulse until well combined. Season with Herbs&Salt and red pepper flakes to taste.
7. Serve with *Panelle* Fries. This aioli is also delicious as a dip for potato fries, with grilled fish, or spread on *panini*.

Pairing suggestion: Prosecco or other sparkling wine

Insalata di Polpo

Octopus Salad

A staple of Sicilian cuisine, *polpo* (octopus) is prepared in many ways and you'll find this salad in restaurants all over the island. Traditionally, recipes call for boiled octopus and boiled potatoes. However, I prefer to sear the octopus on the grill and roast the potatoes in the oven for even more flavor. I also add cherry tomatoes and capers for color and freshness.

Serves 6–8

For the salad:
1 frozen octopus (3 pounds)
2 tablespoons coarse sea salt
1 bay leaf
1 garlic clove, peeled, whole
Juice of 1 lemon
6 Yukon gold Potatoes, peeled and
    cut into 1-inch chunks
Sea salt & freshly ground black pepper
Extra virgin olive oil
2 tablespoons capers, packed in brine
1 cup cherry tomatoes, cut in half
Lemon wedges and parsley for garnish

For the dressing:
Juice of 1 lemon
½ cup extra virgin olive oil
3 garlic cloves, peeled and
    finely minced
¼ cup parsley, finely minced
Sea salt
Michele Ferrante Controne
    Hot Pepper ♥

♥*See favorite products section
on pages 170–176.*

For the octopus:
1. Place frozen octopus in a large pot and cover with water. Add sea salt, bay leave, whole clove of garlic, and lemon juice. Boil until the octopus is tender (about 2 hours). Test every 15–20 minutes by inserting a fork into the thickest part of the tentacles. When the flesh yields (much like a potato), it is finished. Remove from the water and allow to drain.
2. Cut off the tentacles and discard the head. Place tentacles in a large bowl and toss with extra virgin olive oil, then sear on a hot grill until crispy (about 5 minutes on each side).
3. Cut the octopus into ½-inch chunks and place in a serving bowl.

For the potatoes:
4. Preheat oven to 400°F.
5. Place the potato chunks in a bowl, drizzle with olive oil, and season with sea salt and freshly ground pepper to taste. Place on a baking sheet (in a single layer). Bake until tender and slightly browned (about 30 minutes).

For the dressing:
6. Whisk all the dressing ingredients together until well emulsified. Taste and adjust for seasoning.

For the salad:
7. Add the potatoes, cherry tomatoes, and capers to the octopus. Pour the dressing over the salad and mix well. Let the salad rest for 30 minutes or more to allow the flavors to combine.
8. Serve at room temperature with lemon wedges and a sprinkle of fresh parsley. Salad can be refrigerated for up to 1 week.

Pairing suggestion: Grillo or rosato

Pasta alla Norma

Pasta with Fried Eggplant

This wonderfully simple vegetarian pasta is the national dish of Sicily. It probably originated in the city of Catania during the 19th century and is reportedly named after the opera *Norma* by Vincenzo Bellini. Crispy sautéed eggplant over pasta tossed with *Marinara* sauce is delicious, unpretentious, and a perfect example of Sicilian cuisine.

Serves 6–8

Extra virgin olive oil as needed (at least ¾ cup, don't skimp)
1 large eggplant, cut into ¾-inch cubes
Sea salt & freshly ground black pepper
1 large sweet onion, roughly chopped
2 garlic cloves, minced
1 28-ounce can *San Marzano* ♥ tomatoes
1 teaspoon dried oregano, or 1 tablespoon fresh
A few pinches of Michele Ferrante *Controne* Hot Pepper ♥
1-pound pasta (penne, rigatoni, or bucatini), cooked *al dente*
½ cup basil, roughly chopped
½ cup *ricotta salata* cheese, grated (see notes)

♥*See favorite products section on pages 170–176.*

1. Pour oil into a large skillet over medium-high heat and add the eggplant pieces. Do not overcrowd (cook in batches if needed). Sprinkle with sea salt and freshly ground black pepper to taste, adding oil as needed, until nicely browned and soft. Remove to a plate, but do not drain.

2. When finished cooking the eggplant, reserve the oil and leave at least two tablespoons in the skillet. Reduce the heat to medium, add the chopped onion, and cook (for about 5 minutes), then add the garlic and cook until onions are translucent. Add the tomatoes and oregano, along with some sea salt, pepper, and pepper flakes; cook until saucy but not too dry, stirring occasionally. At this point the sauce can be transferred to a food processor and pulsed until blended.

3. Fill a large pot with water, add 1 tablespoon of salt and bring to a boil. Add the pasta and cook until *al dente*. Drain the pasta (reserving the water) and toss with the tomato sauce, gently fold in half of the eggplant and add pasta water as needed until the sauce reaches the desired consistency. Taste and adjust the seasoning, top with the remaining eggplant, basil, and grated cheese, then serve. Pasta can be stored in the refrigerator for up to 1 week.

Pairing suggestion: Rosato or Nero d'Avola

Notes

Ricotta salata is a salted and aged *ricotta* cheese native to Sicily. This cheese is difficult to find in the U.S., but you can substitute *Pecorino Romano* or *Parmigiano-Reggiano* cheese.

Tonno alla Griglia Con Caponata
Grilled Tuna with Caponata

Fresh fish—especially tuna—is available all year 'round in Sicily. I love how this simple marinade pairs so well with the tangy sweetness of the *caponata*. You can also use swordfish or halibut in this recipe.

Serves 6

½ cup extra virgin olive oil
¼ cup lemon juice, freshly squeezed
1 tablespoon fresh lemon zest
3 garlic cloves, minced
3 tablespoons fresh parsley, minced
1 tablespoon fresh oregano, minced
Sea salt & freshly ground black pepper
6 tuna steaks (about 4 ounces each)
Baby arugula
Caponata (recipe on page 164)

1. Combine oil, lemon juice and zest, garlic, parsley, oregano, sea salt, and pepper in a glass dish; mix thoroughly.
2. Add tuna and coat all pieces with the marinade. Refrigerate for 1 hour.
3. Heat grill to medium-high and grill tuna steaks 3 minutes per side.
4. Remove from grill, cover with foil, and allow to rest 5–10 minutes.
5. Serve on a bed of baby arugula topped with *Caponata* (recipe on following page).

Pairing suggestion: Grillo or rosato

Caponata

This appetizer of fried eggplant with peppers, onions, and garlic has been a staple of Sicilian cuisine for centuries. In fact, there are as many variations of this dish as there are kitchens in Sicily! I learned to make this version from a chef in Ortigia and he was adamant about using the proper ingredients and adding them at the appropriate time.

Makes about 4 cups

¾ cup extra virgin olive oil, don't
 skimp, you might need more
2 eggplants, medium diced
1 yellow onion, medium diced
1 red bell pepper, medium diced
1 green bell pepper, medium diced
1 yellow bell pepper, medium diced
2 fresh Roma tomatoes, diced
¼ cup golden raisins, roughly chopped
 (optional)
4 garlic cloves, chopped
2-3 tablespoons capers
3 tablespoons Ritrovo Selections
 Tomato Balsamic Vinegar ♥
3 tablespoons ADI Apicoltura Organic
 Orange Flower Honey ♥ or sugar
¼ cup pine nuts, toasted
½ cup fresh basil, roughly chopped
¼ cup fresh Italian parsley, roughly
 chopped
Sea salt & freshly ground black pepper
Pinch Michele Ferrante *Controne*
 Hot Pepper ♥ (optional)
Parmigiano-Reggiano cheese
 for garnish (optional)

♥*See favorite products section
on pages 170–176.*

1. Heat about ½ of the olive oil (to start) in a large pot. Add the eggplant and onion. Cook for about 10 minutes uncovered. The eggplant should start to release moisture and begin to brown. Stir as needed.
2. Add all of the bell peppers, tomatoes, raisins (if using), garlic, and capers. Stir to combine and cook, covered, for 10 minutes. Uncover and stir, then cook uncovered for another 15–20 minutes until all vegetables are tender.
3. Stir in vinegar and honey (or sugar) and cook for a few minutes more.
4. Turn off the heat and stir in the pine nuts, fresh basil, and parsley.
5. Add red pepper flakes, sea salt, and pepper to taste.
6. Garnish with chopped parsley and a little *Parmigiano-Reggiano* cheese if desired. Serve hot or at room temperature as a salad with bread, or as a condiment for chicken or fish. For a vegetarian meal option, try it with *Panelle* Fries (recipe on page 157).

Blueberry Limoncello Cassata Cake

This cake is one of the best things I have ever made, and I don't even love cake! Traditional Sicilian *Cassata* Cake calls for candied fruit, *ricotta*, and sweet *Marsala* wine. I've substituted fresh blueberries (grown in my own backyard!) and *limoncello* because these summer flavors combine so beautifully. The candied lemon slices are a nod to the original recipe.

Serves 8–12

For the sponge cake:
1¾ cups unbleached all-purpose flour
2 teaspoons cornstarch
1 teaspoon baking powder
½ teaspoon sea salt
6 eggs, separated
2 cups superfine sugar (see notes
    on page 167), divided
1 cup unsalted butter, softened
1 teaspoon vanilla extract
1 teaspoon lemon extract
¾ cup whole milk

For the filling:
30 ounces (2 tubs) whole-milk *ricotta*
2¼ cups confectioners' sugar, sifted
1 teaspoon vanilla extract
1 teaspoon lemon extract
Zest of 2 lemons
2 cups fresh blueberries

For the sponge cake:
1. Preheat oven to 335°F. Prepare three 9-inch round baking pans by greasing each and lining the bottoms with a circle of parchment paper.
2. Add the flour, cornstarch, baking powder, and salt into a large bowl. Whisk to combine and set aside.
3. In a stand mixer fitted with the wire whip attachment, beat the egg whites on high speed to a stiff peak. Add 1 cup of the sugar (about 1 tablespoon at a time) while the mixer is running. Scoop the meringue into a large bowl and set aside.
4. Lightly wipe the mixer bowl and replace the wire whip with the paddle attachment. Cream the butter with the remaining 1 cup of sugar on low speed. Add the vanilla and lemon extracts; mix to combine.
5. Add the egg yolks 1 at a time. Scrape the sides of the bowl all the way to the bottom using a flexible spatula and mix on low speed until the ingredients are thoroughly combined.
6. Alternately add the flour mixture and the milk about ¼ at a time without pausing between additions.
7. Stop the mixer and gently fold the meringue into the batter with a flexible spatula, about ⅓ at a time. (To fold, drag your spatula around the edge of the bowl and fold over the middle of the batter. Repeat this motion until the batter and meringue are fully mixed.) Pour the mixture evenly into the 3 prepared pans and bake for 25–30 minutes, or until the cake bounces back when lightly pressed and a wooden toothpick inserted in the center comes out clean.
8. Cool the cakes for about 5 minutes, then run a knife around the edges and invert the cakes onto a cooling rack and gently peel off of the parchment paper. They will be fragile, so handle them with care.

For the filling:
9. In a stand mixer fitted with the wire whip attachment, whip the *ricotta*, sifted confectioners' sugar, and vanilla and lemon extracts until creamy (2–3 minutes). Stir in the lemon zest and the blueberries and set aside.

Recipe continues on page 167.

For the frosting:
2 cups heavy whipping cream
⅓ cup confectioners' sugar, sifted
1 teaspoon *limoncello*

For the candied lemon slices:
2 lemons, washed and cut into
⅛-inch slices
2 tablespoons lemon juice, freshly
squeezed
1 cup sugar
¾ cup water

To assemble:
¼ cup *limoncello*
1 cup fresh blueberries
Candied lemon slices
Mint leaves

Notes

Make your own super-fine sugar by placing granulated sugar in the bowl of a food processor and pulsing until it is a fine powder.

For the frosting:
10. In a stand mixer fitted with the wire whip attachment, whip the heavy cream and sifted confectioners' sugar until stiff peaks form. Add the *limoncello* and mix until just incorporated. Store in the refrigerator until needed, up to 3 days.

For the candied lemon slices:
11. Combine the lemon juice, sugar, and water in a large skillet; heat until the sugar is melted. Add the lemon slices in a single layer; do not overlap. Boil for about 25–40 minutes until the lemons are translucent. Use tongs to flip the lemon slices over about halfway through. It can take a while, so be patient.
12. Remove lemons and set on baking tray lined with parchment paper. Reserve the lemon syrup for another use, like a lemon drop cocktail!
13. Refrigerate lemon slices for several hours before using. Use them to garnish desserts or cocktails. They are sweet, sour, and delicious.

To assemble:
14. Place 1 layer of cake on a plate and brush with *limoncello*. Spread with ½ of the *ricotta* filling. Top with another cake round, brush with *limoncello*, and spread the remainder of the filling, brush the last cake round with *limoncello* and place on top. At this point it is helpful to refrigerate the cake for a few hours (up to overnight) to allow the *ricotta* filling to set before frosting. If you have a 9-inch springform cake pan to arrange your cake in, it makes this process a little easier. Place a sheet of parchment on the bottom of the spring-form pan and allow the edges to protrude beyond the rim before locking the pan in place. This forms a little collar around the cake that will make it easy to transfer to a serving platter. Trim off the excess parchment once the cake is on the final serving dish.
15. Once the *ricotta* mixture is set, frost with the whipped cream frosting. It can be piped or spread with an offset spatula. Top with blueberries, candied lemon slices, and mint sprigs. Cake can be covered and refrigerated for up to 1 week. It is actually really delicious after it sits for a few days—if it lasts that long.

Pairing suggestion: Limoncello, of course!

Limoncello

Fun and easy to make, *limoncello* is also a great excuse for a party! Simply buy a bunch of lemons at your local warehouse store, and ask everyone to bring their own vegetable peelers, vodka, and storage jars. If you plan the party in the fall, the *limoncello* will be ready for holiday or hostess gifts.

Makes about 3 liters of Limoncello

15–20 lemons (see notes)
2 bottles (750 ml) 100-proof vodka
   (see notes)
4 cups sugar
5 cups water

Notes

If you can find Meyer lemons, they have luscious flavor. However other lemons can be used as well.

Use 100-proof vodka (if you can find it), which has less flavor than lower proof spirits. Also, the high alcohol level will ensure that the *limoncello* will not turn to ice in the freezer. But I have also used 80-proof vodka or Everclear with good results.

1. Wash lemons with a vegetable brush and hot water to remove any residue of pesticides or wax, then dry the lemons.
2. Carefully zest the lemons with a zester or vegetable peeler, making sure that no white pith is included. (The pith, the white part underneath the rind, is too bitter and will spoil your *limoncello*.)
3. In a 1-gallon glass jar, pour 1 bottle of vodka and add the lemon zest. Shake to insure that all the lemon rinds are covered in vodka.
4. Cover the jar and let sit in a cool dark place at room temperature for 30–40 days. The longer it rests, the better the taste will be. (There is no need to stir—all you have to do is wait.) As the *limoncello* sits, the vodka slowly takes on the flavor and the lovely yellow color of the lemon rind. After allowing the vodka and lemons to infuse for 30-40 days, move on to step 5.
5. In a large saucepan set over medium heat, combine the sugar and water. Cook until sugar is melted and mixture is slightly thickened, approximately 5–7 minutes. Let the syrup cool before adding to the vodka and lemon rind mixture in the glass jar. Add the second bottle of vodka and allow to steep for another 30–40 days.
6. Strain and compost the lemon peels (the peels can also be frozen for up to 6 months and used in breads or cakes). Transfer *limoncello* into sterilized bottles; use recycled bottles with cork stoppers. Store in the freezer indefinitely. Serve well chilled.

Limoncello

Favorite Products

Extra Virgin Olive Oil

It is no secret that I prefer Italian olive oil. Much like wine, the *terroir* of the groves determines the quality and flavor of the oil. From mild to herbaceous to spicy, olive oil possesses unique profiles. Extra virgin olive oil is defined by an oil with excellent flavor and aroma with a free fatty acid content of not more than 0.8 g per 100 g (0.8%); extra virgin olive oil is always first- and cold-pressed ("First Press" and "Cold Pressed" labels are merely marketing buzz words). The olive oils listed here are estate olive oils imported by Ritrovo Selections (*ritrovo.com*). I have visited the farms in Italy and met the families who produce these superior oils. Look for them at *CookingWithPoggiBonsi.com* and other specialty retailers.

CASINA ROSSA EXTRA VIRGIN OLIVE OIL

Region: Abruzzo. Estate produced.
Varietals: *Gentile*, *Intosso*, and *Ghiandaro*
Deep green in color with a slightly grassy and fruity aroma and fruity, herbaceous flavors. Blends beautifully in dressings and sauces.

CASINA ROSSA EXTRA VIRGIN OLIVE OIL WITH SICILIAN LEMON

Region: Abruzzo
Varietals: *Gentile*, *Intosso*, and *Ghiandaro* olives pressed directly with 100% Sicilian lemons.
A "dressing in a jar" made for green salads, seafood, and marinades. Handles heat well and is ideal for sautéing vegetables.

CASINA ROSSA EXTRA VIRGIN OLIVE OIL WITH BLACK TRUFFLE

Region: Abuzzo
Varietals: *Gentile*, *Intosso*, and *Ghiandaro* olives infused with genuine black truffles from Abruzzo.
Alluring fruit-herb balance makes for a versatile oil. It's also delightful drizzled on freshly popped popcorn.

COLLI ETRUSCHI

Region: Lazio
Varietal: 100% *Caninese* olives
Bold, fruity, and versatile. Perfect for salads and drizzling on bread. The unique amphora bottle makes it a lovely gift for the chef in your life.

MARINO FAMILY EXTRA VIRGIN OLIVE OIL

Region: Sicily. Estate produced and bottled in the Monte Iblei zone of southeastern Sicily.
Varietals: 100% *Tonda Iblea* olives
Early-harvest, certified organic, and small-batch grown in a carpet of wild herbs which gives the oil a wonderful herbal flavor that pairs well will Sicilian dishes, especially eggplant and roasted vegetables.

POGGI BONSI EXTRA VIRGIN OLIVE OIL BY TRAMPETTI

Region: Umbria
Varietals: *Leccino* and *Frantoio*
From olive groves on the Spoletto Assisi hills, "Gold Coast of Olive Oil." Slightly fruity and grassy with a fine fruit-herb balance. A chef's staple that is great for cooking as well as finishing.

TRAMPETTI ORGANIC EXTRA VIRGIN OLIVE OIL

Region: Umbria
Varietals: 100% *Moraiolo*
Organic olive oil with an herbal and slightly earthy aroma. Fluid and light on the palate. Fruity, green apple flavor with a slight bitterness. Full peppery finish. Best as a finishing oil.

Favorite Products

Balsamic Vinegar

Modena is a city in northern Italy known for balsamic vinegar production. Balsamic vinegar is made from grape "must" (concentrated grape juice) that is boiled down to a syrup and aged for several years in a succession of wooden barrels. (For detailed information, visit the consortium website: *ConsorzioBalsamico.it*). Most of the vinegars listed here are imported by Ritrovo Selections *(ritrovo.com)* and are made with grape must flavored with apples, cherries, citrus, and tomato juice. They are available from *CookingWithPoggiBonsi.com* and other specialty retailers.

EDMOND FALLOT WALNUT VINEGAR

Made in Dijon, France, this walnut vinegar (not a balsamic) is tangy with just the right touch of nutty flavor. Great for everyday green salads or drizzled on grilled meats. *Imported by TheFrenchFarm.com.*
Substitution: Apple cider or white wine vinegar.

RITROVO SELECTIONS AGED BALSAMIC

Sofi™ Gold Award Winner.* Excellently balanced and versatile IGP Certified *Balsamico* of Modena. Produced from *Lambrusco* and *Trebbiano* grape must, and oak-barrel-aged. A perfect match for grilled and roasted meats, aged cheeses, and salad dressings.
Substitution: Your favorite aged balsamic vinegar.

RITROVO SELECTIONS ORGANIC APPLE BALSAMIC

A Sofi™ Gold Award Winner. Juicy, tart organic *Trentino* apples and organic Modena grape must are combined to create this balanced, yet luscious vinegar. Wonderful in salad dressings, especially with pears, apples and walnuts. Delightful with aged and blue cheeses.
Substitution: Your favorite aged balsamic vinegar.

RITROVO SELECTIONS ORGANIC TOMATO BALSAMIC

This vinegar is made in Italy with flavorful tomato juice paired with crystalline white grape must. With just the right sweet-savory balance. It's delicious in anything with tomatoes such as tomato jams and *Romesco* Sauce.
Substitution: Your favorite red wine vinegar.

RITROVO SELECTIONS ORGANIC CHERRY BALSAMIC

This bright and juicy vinegar is a balance of sweet grape must and rich Amarena cherry juice. Use on salads with mixed greens and cherries, or radicchio and duck *confit*. Lovely over ice cream, pie, or cobbler—especially with fresh cherries. It is wonderful in cocktails too.
Substitution: Your favorite aged balsamic vinegar.

RITROVO SELECTIONS ORGANIC CITRUS BALSAMIC

Inspired by the sun-drenched lemon groves of Sorrento, this lively balsamic vinegar is an enticing blend of organic lemon juice, *Trebbiano* grape must and wine vinegar. Delightful in salads and drizzled on vegetables.
Substitution: Your favorite white balsamic vinegar and a squeeze of lemon juice.

RITROVO SELECTIONS WHITE BALSAMIC

Made in Modena from locally sourced *Trebbiano* white grape must and white wine vinegar. Perfectly balanced with light acidity. A go-to pantry item. It's delicious in all types of vinaigrettes and for making pickles, marinades, or fruit shrubs.
Substitution: Your favorite white balsamic vinegar.

*Sofi™ Awards honor the best and most innovative products in specialty food.

Favorite Products

Honey, Salts, Spices, and More

Flavored salts and spice blends are a wonderful way to infuse flavor into even the simplest of dishes. Tuscan honey, "00" flour, DOP *San Marzano* tomatoes, and *taggiasca* olives round out the selection of my favorite products, most of which are imported by Ritrovo Selections (*ritrovo.com*). *CookingWithPoggiBonsi.com,* as well as other specialty retailers, sell these items.

ADI APICOLTURA
ORGANIC ORANGE FLOWER HONEY

White gold and spreadable, this honey is as distinctive in appearance as it is in flavor. Springtime aromas of citrus and white flowers are immediately apparent, but not overwhelming. Try it in baking, in black or green tea, drizzled over *ricotta* cheese, or on scones and biscuits.
Substitution: Your favorite honey.

CASINA ROSSA
HERBS&SALT

An aromatic blend of Adriatic Sea salt and herbs from throughout the Italian Peninsula, this pantry staple makes a perfect rub for grilled steak, chicken, or prawns. This is my go-to salt for meats, soups, and pasta sauces.
Substitution: Equal parts of sea salt and your favorite Italian seasoning.

CASINA ROSSA
FIORI&SALT

A beautiful mix of sea salt, wild orange peel, and ten types of edible flowers. This salt works beautifully with fresh *ricotta* or *burrata* cheeses, and sprinkled on green salads and puréed soups.
Substitution: Sea salt.

CASINA ROSSA
SALT&SALUTÈ DIGESTIVO

This infused salt incorporates super-fruit berries, Italian digestive herbs and spices like juniper, fennel, and cardamom to bring pleasant aromatics to red meats and venison. It is an excellent salt for dressings, pies, cobblers, and for finishing chocolate desserts.
Substitution: Sea salt.

CASINA ROSSA
TRUFFLE&SALT

A Sofi™ Gold Award Winner.* This international sensation was the first "truffle salt" in the world market. A heady and aromatic blend of Italian black truffle and sea salt. Delicious with mushrooms, cheeses, pasta, and even popcorn.
Substitution: 8 parts sea salt, 1 part dried black truffle.

CASINA ROSSA
SAFFRON&SALT

Sea salt blended with delicate strands of saffron. The golden hue and delicate flavor enhance fusion cuisine, *risotto* or fresh *ricotta* cheese. It is also lovely with seafood, rice dishes, and Spanish cuisine.
Substitution: 8 parts sea salt, 1 part saffron threads.

CASINA ROSSA
SALT SAMPLER

A selection of six mini salts, this sampler is a fun and economical way to try them all. Sampler includes Truffle&Salt, Fennel&Salt, Saffron&Salt, Fiori&Salt, Porcini&Salt, and Herbs&Salt. It makes a perfect gift for the chef in your life.

FIOR DI MAIELLA
SPICY BRUSCHETTA SALT

This is an expert blend of aromatic Italian herbs and spices including parsley, chili pepper, red pepper, basil, thyme, garlic, and sage. Add it to pasta, dipping olive oils, vegetables, and meatballs.
Substitution: Equal parts of your favorite Italian seasoning, sea salt, and red pepper flakes.

FIOR DI MAIELLA
SMOKED SWEET PEPPER POWDER

Pepperoni Dolce di Altino is a regional sweet pepper found in Abruzzo, Italy. Fior di Maiella adds a layer of flavor by naturally smoking it before grinding into a fine powder. Elegant and complex—it is the perfect addition to traditional Italian and Spanish dishes. *Substitution: Spanish sweet smoked paprika.*

TAGGIASCA OLIVES

Typical olive of the *Riviera Ligure* region, known as the "Italian Riviera." They are buttery, compact, and tender, with a low sodium content. These olives complement seafood, meat and poultry dishes, salads, pizza, and are delicious in *tapanade*.
Substitution: Kalamata or other black olives.

MICHELE FERRANTE
CONTRONE HOT PEPPER

Air-dried, hand-ground hot pepper from Campania. Zesty yet nutty flavor with notes of wood smoke and plenty of heat. Wonderful with pasta and bean dishes. *Substitution: Your favorite red pepper flakes.*

MOLINO VERRINI
100% ITALIAN WHEAT FLOUR TYPE "00"

"00" flour is Italian milled flour that is used for pasta and pastry making. You will find that this is also called "*Doppio Zero*" which means "double zero" in Italian. The grading system is 2, 1, 0 or 00, indicating how finely ground the flour is and how much of the bran and germ have been removed. It is a finely ground all-purpose flour. The Verrini family carries on the generations-old tradition of producing the highest quality flours in the province of Modena and Reggio Emilia.
Substitution: Another brand of "00" flour or unbleached all-purpose flour.

DOP SAN MARZANO TOMATOES

Nothing can compare with *San Marzano* tomatoes grown in the Mediterranean sun, especially in southern Italy. They are a little more expensive than domestic canned tomatoes (typically $6–$7 for a 28-ounce can), but they are so worth it when you taste the rich, thick, and sumptuous sauces full of sweet tomato flavor.

What are DOP San Marzano Tomatoes?
San Marzano is both a type of tomato and a region in Italy. The *San Marzano* tomato is a type of plum tomato which is longer and thinner than the typical plum tomato. It is also less acidic and has thicker flesh, fewer seeds, and a sweeter taste. I know it can be confusing in the grocery store because not all canned tomatoes from Italy are *San Marzano*, and *San Marzano* tomatoes are grown outside of Italy too, including in the U.S.

DOP stands for the Italian designation *Denominazione d'Origine Protetta* (Protected Designation of Origin in English). The DOP certification was developed to protect the reputation of the regional foods and eliminate the unfair competition by non-genuine products, which may be of inferior quality or with a different flavor. DOP *San Marzano* Tomatoes are grown in volcanic soil in the shadow of Mount Vesuvius in the in small town of *San Marzano* sul Sarno, near Naples, Italy.

Look for the DOP designation and seal on the back of the can. Each can is numbered to ensure its authenticity. They are not sold at *CookingWithPoggiBonsi.com*, but they can be found at specialty grocery stores and other online retailers.
Substitution: Another brand of canned tomatoes.

*Sofi™ Awards honor the best and most innovative products in specialty food.

Plan your dream

poggibonsitours.com

POGGIBONSI

Index